FUNDAMENTAL MISCONCEPTIONS OF BIBLE BASICS

A Search For Spiritual Truth and Moral Purity

F. Steward Bartlett

Published by
Lulu Enterprises
860 Aviation Parkway, Ste. 300
Morrisville, NC 27560

Copyright © 2008 by F. Steward Bartlett

All rights reserved. No part of this book may be reproduced or transmitted in any form or by any means, electronic or mechanical, including photocopying, recording, or by any information storage and retrieval system, except where permitted by law.

ISBN Number: 978-0-615-25704-4

Printed in the United States of America

Dedication

This book is dedicated to God's Will, which has been my greatest source of strength and comfort throughout.

It is also dedicated to all those who have the courage of their convictions to search out the truth, verify it, and be brave enough to proclaim it boldly.

INDEX

Chapter	Subject	Page
	Acknowledgements	v
	Introduction	vii
	The Bible By Parts	xv
1.	Practical Arrangement of the Bible	1
2.	Salvation and Apostleship are Inseparable	25
3.	A Seal of the Righteousness of Faith	36
4.	Hebrews – The Unique Epistle	66
5.	First a Wife...or a Christian	78
6.	Six Reasons for Departing	128
7.	Opinion, Option, and Expediency	172
	Final Word	235

ACKNOWLEDGEMENTS

Special thanks are offered for the valued assistance of everyone who contributed simply by their awareness of this effort. An extra measure of gratitude is offered to Max Goins who was the minister at the First Christian Church of Marianna, Arkansas during the early stages of this writing. His assistance included openness and freedom with his thoughts regardless of his personal opinion. His added input in everything from organizing thoughts into words, to chapter layouts, has proven invaluable.

My friend, Barbara H, provided priceless assistance in lending virgin ears to this type of material. As an avid reader, her understanding of phrasing and editing has been an added asset. Her help and friendship has been incalculable in putting on the finishing touches.

My spouse has been deprived of time and attention many times while this effort was in progress. This could not have been accomplished without that patience. My children have given the most wonderful encouragement when blank walls loomed and discouragement set in.

Sisters, Louise, Ann and Ruth, along with numerous friends, have provided the element of 'the great expectation' for the finished work. Louise, worked long and diligent hours editing while trying to say what I wanted to say, renewing her computer skills, and learning the techniques involved in getting this book to the online publisher. I couldn't have accomplished this without her.

The critics have proven invaluable either by spoken criticism or their silence. Both spurred new conviction to complete this work.

To everyone with whom there has been contact in any way, a heartfelt 'thank you' is offered. For all this and more, eternal gratitude is due God the Father and the Lord Jesus Christ. The reference material is from the King James Version with occasional references to the Revised Version.

INTRODUCTION

The intended purpose of this book is to encourage readers to read the Bible, to become ardent students of God's word and to remove oneself from human influence and ideology. It is important to read this book in sequence to gain a better perspective of the order and the laws.

Many people think they are unable to gain an understanding of the Bible without the aid of a college educated professional. But these professionals are paid by the people they teach.

It has been this writer's unhappy experience that teachers of religion won't discuss certain Bible topics willingly or without bias. These subjects are necessary foundational elements that will give a clear and easy path to understanding God's Word. Therefore, the primary effort of this work is to create an unbiased interest and ability in Bible understanding.

This is a study of moral and spiritual issues that are not allowed in-depth study. The topics under consideration are at the very base of the faith and practice that is acceptable to the Father of Heaven and earth, before whom we shall all give an account.

Everyone can (Note I Corinthians 1:26) acquire the correct understanding of God's Word because the Bible is written on or near the sixth grade reading level. As a general rule, it is not the educated or powerful that accept the faith, but the poor, the common people. (Acts 4:13)

Every Scripture agrees, explains, and supports other Scriptures. Everything connects and none stand alone as a one time event. Full faith demands that if we believe Christ we must also believe He will show us the Way. We must fervently desire faith for it to become reality.

Gaining a solid foundation in the written word involves realizing the divisions and parts as admonished in II Timothy 2:15. These divisions include spiritual laws and moral laws: These are the two laws found within any time period. Basically, the commandments of the Spirit teach worship and respect for God as the only God.

Moral concepts teach respect for each other as mortals of equal standing before God.

The two laws are closely intertwined in the written word and are hardly distinguishable in the usual manner of reading and comprehension. Recognizing the idea of God's spiritual guidelines is of the utmost necessity in bringing order to a chaotic religious situation.

Spiritual commands and guidelines are set in a positive frame. These are the laws of worship and reverence and which we owe Him as our God.

The old law gives the precepts in a kind of continual flow as to a child. The law of worship and the new law are presented in more of a narrative form as when speaking to a more adult mentality. The act of adding to, subtracting from, and/or rearrangement of God's spiritual laws gives us the divided and confused religious situation we have today.

The Bible is a book that gives witness to itself. Every statement in the Bible supports and verifies every other statement. This work gives quotes directly from the Bible to present proof of that support and verification. **It is important to have a Bible close at hand for reference purposes when reading this book.** Reading directly from the Bible gives additional information and a solid base.

Many are the millions who believe in the Lord Jesus Christ as the Saviour of the world. Yet few realize the matter of SPIRITUAL SIN. Moral sin is hardly recognized in this day and time, and spiritual sin has not been dealt with in any degree, during any time period, since the times of the Apostles.

SPIRITUAL SIN is defined as the changing of God's laws of worship, the changing of the conditions to be met to realize salvation, the changing of how we are to relate and worship God. These laws are not recognized and respected as a reality to be dealt with. These are the things of the Spirit, the carnally unseen.

SPIRITUAL SIN is just as much wickedness and evil as moral sin, yet it is never allowed discussion or debate. This is all in the name of tolerance and respect for the ideas, reasoning, and feelings of various "spiritual leaders", of various and differing abilities and stations. The Lord is quoted as telling Pontius Pilate, the ruler of Judea, "My kingdom is not of this world". But people want the church guided and ruled according to the tenants of the world.

As a result, we have an endless number of beliefs and practices along with mass confusion created by the differing doctrines. Consequently, no one religious doctrine can show a complete and wholesome doctrine, with proven accuracy that does not, in some way add to, subtract from, or contradict the written word.

Most believers do not search the Scriptures seriously. Because of this lack of personal investigation, the importance of eternal salvation from eternal destruction is not grasped as being a solid fact.

Daily living and demands also press down upon us until it is easy to neglect that which does not command our immediate attention and energy. The "seen" takes precedence over the "unseen". It is human nature to leave some things to others whom we may feel are more qualified, even when there are possible misgivings and doubts. This is the danger. This is the destruction.

This work seeks to bring forward the points of doctrine that are so woefully neglected and ignored by those who claim to teach the truth in specific detail, and by the religious world as a whole.

In my twenty year sincere, wholehearted commitment and association with the CHURCHES OF CHRIST, there came a time of questioning concerning one point of their doctrine. Having found answers by research of the Scriptures, I presented these findings to various members of the local church. Their rejection of these presentations was immediate with no hesitation or consideration.

Dating from 1975, a diligent, enduring study has been undertaken to find conclusive answers to several questions. This book discusses these violations of Scriptural doctrine among the various religious teachings, with the conclusions confirmed and verified by quotations provided from the written Word.

Some subjects, appearing to be the essence of simplicity, are sometimes difficult to put into explanation without a certain degree of involved discussion. The apparent simplicity is part of the reason they are never subjected to thorough investigation.

These subjects are discussed regularly in Bible classes and in Sunday sermons. Still, it seems that the precise points are never realized. The difficulty in realizing the need to study these particular points appears to be related to the use of familiar and elementary language, words and terms used in every day speaking.

Discussion in this endeavor is rather involved in relation to the subject matter. This became necessary because of the many questions of profound doubt and solid complacency in long-held beliefs. The great problem comes in finding a means to initiate investigation by the mind that is already thoroughly convinced and comfortable with those long-held beliefs.

Having a lack of natural writing desire and ability, There were many instances of indecision felt by this writer as to the worth of completing this work. But the concept could not be explained in casual or impromptu discussion. Answers to questions were never quite comprehended. It seems there is a total disbelief that any element could be missing in the commonly accepted doctrines of the believers of Christ. Thus, the same questions arise again and again. Many of these same believers show a strong unwillingness to investigate the possibility that their faith is not quite as complete as they imagined. This made oral explanation virtually ineffective.

Note: There have been charges of redundancy in occasional previews of this material, as well a arguments against the ideas presented. Yet no proof texts are offered either way. Obviously this is a matter of sensation and feeling, with nothing based in fact. The references, words, and phrases are very familiar to those who attend preaching and Bible study sessions. To delve into these same Scriptures in a complete and connected manner, rather than the usual hit or miss, is to search out the unfamiliar and possibly leave a feeling of discomfort and uncertainty. In religious circles, maintaining a safe and contented state is the key to maintaining the status quo; the watchwords being content and secure, otherwise known as complacency.

"Then I said, I will not make mention of him, nor speak any more in his name. But his word was in mine heart as a burning fire shut up in my bones, and I was weary with forbearing, and I could not stay." (Jeremiah 20:9)

THE BIBLE BY PARTS

1.
Old Testament
Our World in its Beginning
The Lineage of Christ

2.
New Testament Beginning with
Matthew, Mark, Luke, John

3.
Acts 2 Shows Commands and Examples
For Salvation with Continuance of the
Body of Christ
Colossians 1:24

4.
Example and Command
The Next 21 Books Show the
Perfect Way of a Life in Christ
Romans 6, Galatians 3:27

5.
Revelation: The Third Time Period
In Prophetic Form
Bringing the Earth to an End
Revelation 22

Note: The Three Ages Had Beginning Miracles
    1. Genesis 1-8
    2. Exodus through Joshua
    3. Matthew through Acts

Chapter One

THE PRACTICAL ARRANGEMENT OF THE BIBLE

Study to Show Thyself Approved

The Patriarchal Law and the Law of Moses
As Concurrent Laws

Two Laws – Two Time Periods
Both Authoritative Laws

CHAPTER ONE

THE PRACTICAL ARRANGEMENT OF THE BIBLE

Since the time of the sin in the Garden of Eden, God has provided guidance for the conduct of living, counsel in forgiveness of sin, and instruction in how he is to be reverenced.

Instruction for everything from God to man is found in the book from the God of heaven. This book, commonly known as the Bible, contains a smooth and quiet order. The constantly maintained and peaceful course is often passed by unnoticed. This is due, in part, to the fact that the revealed laws of obedience are relatively short. (Matthew 22: 37-40) Man is hindered by his inability to understand and unwillingness to obey God's righteousness. Because of human inability, God's will is given throughout the ages through three time periods. These three time periods are known as Patriarchal, Mosaic, and Christian.

Each respective dispensation brings instruction suitable to the ability of men to accept and obey. The admonition from the Apostle Paul is appropriate. "Study to show thy self approved unto God, a workman that needeth not to be ashamed, rightly dividing the word of truth. (II Timothy 2:15). Understanding the principles of each time period with its implications, adds much to comprehending and profiting from the total written Word.

Along with recognizing the time periods, there are vital keys, or points of understanding, to consider in each part of the Bible. Key points are very important to the opening of doors and to understanding many situations. But first, the key must be recognized. These elements are positioned in exact and essential order, with this order being an important study within itself.

To become acquainted with the practical arrangement of the Bible is to see the plan and purpose of the Bible at a glance. This one thing would greatly increase the fulfillment of the plea of the Apostles:

"Now I beseech you, brethren, by the name of our Lord Jesus Christ, that you all speak the same thing, and that there be no divisions among you; that you be perfectly joined together in the same mind and in the same judgment"....not in the words which man's wisdom teaches, but which the holy spirit teaches; comparing spiritual things with spiritual."(I Corinthians 1:10, 2:13)

Realizing the overall plan of the Bible would end much of the religious division among those believing in Jesus Christ as Lord and Saviour.

In beginning any examination of the various parts of the Bible, the Old Testament and New Testament are the first to be brought to our attention. Within each of the testaments are the covenants from God to men for the respective time.

Within the Old Testament, the first law given to men is known as the Patriarchal Law. Following the sin in the Garden of Eden, the Lord gave his commandments to the family fathers. Noah of the sixth and seventh chapters of Genesis, and Abraham in the twelfth chapter, are examples of this law. The Patriarchal law is not given in a detailed written record. However, there is no doubt of the existence of this covenant because of the evidence shown by the examples of faith found in such people as Able, Enoch, Noah, Abraham and Job. God spoke about the practical covenant as a solid fact saying that **"Abraham obeyed** my voice and kept my charges, my commandments, my statutes, and my laws". (Genesis 26:5)

In this same reading, Abimblech, King of the Philistines, was very aware of righteousness and unrighteousness. Note verses six through eleven. There were always guidelines from God to men.

Among those not listed in the Jewish nation or in the lineage of Christ Jesus, is a notable example of a man of faith who was obedient to the Patriarchal law. The man's name is Hiram, the King of Tyre. Without being a part of the Hebrew nation, he is shown as a man with great respect for God's plan and the people included in it.

"Then Hiram the King of Tyre answered in writing, when he sent to Solomon, Because the Lord hath loved his people, he hath made thee king over them. Hiram said moreover, Blessed be the Lord God of Israel, that made heaven and earth, who hath given to David the king a wise son, endued with prudence and understanding, that might build a house for the Lord and an house for his kingdom." (II Chronicles 2:11-12)

From the above reading, it appears the people of that day, whether Hebrew or Gentile, understood the position of both nations and the plan of God in each case. It seems their understanding was much better than that which is shown by most Bible students, even with the present day benefit of hindsight.

The New Testament also testifies to the faith of the people during the patriarchal law. One of these can be found in the book of Hebrews.
"By faith Abel offered unto God a more excellent sacrifice than Cain, by which he obtained witness that he was righteous, God testifying of his gifts: and by it he being dead yet speaketh." (Hebrews 11:4).

In the first recorded letter to Christians we find it written;
"So then faith cometh by hearing, and hearing by the word of God." (Romans 10:17). Able heard and obeyed. Cain heard, but did not obey".

The patriarch, Job, is shown as a man of faith without the Law of Moses.
"There was a man in the land of Uz, whose name was Job; and that man was perfect and upright, and one that feared God and eschewed evil. And there were born unto him seven sons and three daughters...Job sent and sanctified them, and rose up early in the morning, and offered burnt offerings according to the number of them all: for Job said, It may be that my sons have sinned, and cursed

God in their hearts. Thus did Job continually." (Job 1:1-5).

"Behold, we count them happy which endure. Ye have heard of the patience of Job, and have seen the end of the Lord: that the Lord is very pitiful, and of tender mercy." (James 5:11). The faith of God was taught to the patriarchs if they desired to hear it.

It is apparent that the majority of Gentile nations gave themselves over to idolatry during the time the Law of Moses was in effect. But that did not change the commandments with which they were charged. Neither does it change the fact of those individuals who were faithful to God within that law.

The patriarchal commandments were in effect until the time of the law of Christ. In the course of this law there were promises given to the fathers of the coming of Christ.

"For the promise, that he should be the heir of the world, was not to Abraham, or to his seed, through the law but through the righteousness of faith." (Romans 4:13).

With the call of Abraham in Genesis 12, the family through whom the Saviour was to come, was separated. Four hundred and thirty years after the calling of

Abraham the Law of Moses was confirmed to the children of Israel. (Galatians 3:17).

With the delivering of the Law of Moses, there also came the knowledge of sin and the penalty in each instance. The Old Law was not an instrument of salvation and confirmation; rather an instrument of promise and a shadow of things to come. The ninth and tenth chapters of Hebrews demonstrate these things in terms which cannot be disputed.(Hebrews 10:1)

But many religious people place great confidence in an eternal value of the Law of Moses where God has not done so. Evidence of excessive value placed in the Law of Moses is seen in the time of Christ with the continuing effort of the Jew to proselyte the Gentile. The religious believers of that time could not imagine pleasing God without being subject to that law. Also, after the proclamation of the gospel message of Jesus, the Law of Moses continued to have great importance for a great many people. The fifteenth chapter of Acts gives witness of "certain men who came down from Judea which taught the brethren, and said, Except you are circumcised after the manner of Moses, ye cannot be saved."

It is evident that there are great numbers of people who hold a strong

belief in an ongoing quality of salvation within the Law of Moses or the Old Testament commandments. This is especially true of the Ten Commandments. The books of Galatians and Hebrews go into great detail showing the place and purpose of the Old Law and New Law. Each have a time and purpose. The Old Law is the carnal or material law pointing to the pattern of the spiritual Truth that was to follow. (Hebrews 9:24)
"For Christ is not entered into the holy places made with hands, which are the figures of the true; but into heaven itself, now to appear in the presence of God for us."

The introduction of the Law of Moses did not interfere with the Patriarchal Law or the people who were subject to it. Christ Jesus was as much a promise and expectation to the Gentile as he was to the Jew. Witness the wise men who came from the east. These men were wise men, yet they had to rely on the Jewish scribes in their search for the Christ Child. (Matthew 2) There are other instances in which Jesus was sought by those of the Gentile nations. (John 12:20).

Even after the resurrection of the Lord, a man of Caesarea who was not Jewish, is credited with, "being a devout man and one that feared God with all his house, which gave much alms to the people, and prayed to God always". (Acts 10:11)

The Apostle wrote in Romans concerning the Gentiles and the Law of Moses, "For as many as have sinned without the law shall also perish without law; and as many as have sinned in the law shall be judged by the law; (For not the hearers of the law are just before God, but the doers of the law shall be justified. For when the Gentiles, which have not the law, do by nature the things contained in the law, these, having not the law, are a law unto themselves, which show the work of the law written in their hearts, their conscience also bearing witness, and their thoughts the mean while accusing or else excusing one another;") (Romans 2:12-15)

At this point we have two laws with neither one infringing upon the other: The patriarchal law, which began with the exit from the garden and ended with the proclamation of the law of Christ in Acts 2. Then we have the Law of Moses beginning at Mount Sinai and ending also with the proclamation of the law of Christ in Acts 2. The Patriarchal Law and the Law of Moses were concurrent.

The second major part of the Bible is the New Testament. This part also has distinct, pivotal, points with essential guidelines showing the intent of God's word in clarity and simplicity.

The first four books of Matthew, Mark, Luke, and John are unique within themselves. In John, the last book of the four, the stated purpose of these books is given: "And many other signs truly did Jesus in the presence of his disciples, which are not written in this book: but these are written, that ye might believe that Jesus is the Christ, the son of God; and that believing ye might have life through his name." This is the intent and purpose of these four books. Each writer contributes parts of the life and teachings of Jesus, some different from the other writers and some the same. Without fear of contradiction it can be said that since John did not reveal all Jesus said and did, the three other witnesses to the deity of Christ did not do otherwise.

During the Lord's tenure on earth, moral and spiritual principles were given, but the promised kingdom with the accompanying rule of law, was always seen as being 'at hand'. In the study of the teachings of Christ while on the earth, it is essential to become aware of which law any particular point relates. Everything the Lord taught related either to the Old Law, the coming New Law, or both.

It is often thought that when Jesus would quote from the Old Law, followed by, "But I say unto you...", that he was contrasting the old and the new laws. Closer examination will show that he is enlarging and expanding the greater depths of understanding to be found between and within both laws. Matthew 5, 6, and 7, the Sermon on the Mount, is an example of timeless principles examined in the light of both old and new Laws. The occasions of these teachings explored the spiritual connections to the more familiar moral laws.

Occasions for the majority of teaching which related to the Law of Moses were in answer to accusations against the Lord by the Pharisees and Sadducees. The ruling sector feared the power of Jesus with the general population. Because of this fear, healings on the Sabbath day were a favorite issue in their efforts to discredit the power of Jesus, with plans to ultimately destroy him and his doctrine. People in high places derive their power and economy from people in low places. Any threat to this safety net is met with aggressive measures. No difference is displayed in this instance.

Jesus Christ was not the king they had fervently expected, with the hope of high office in his kingdom. It was on one of these occasions in which the Lord asked his accusers, "How can ye believe, which receive honor one of another, and seek not the honor that cometh from God only?" Then the Lord warned them, "Do not think that I will accuse you to the Father: there is one that accuseth you, even Moses, in whom ye trust. For had ye believed Moses, you would have believed me: for he wrote of me. But if ye believe not his writing, how shall ye believe my words?" (John 5:45)

The unbelieving element did not believe, nor practice the Law they professed to follow. Therefore they could not believe the teachings of Christ in relation to the New Law. Because of their resistance toward him, Jesus taught them about the coming kingdom (church) by way of parables. The things taught to them in relation to their questions about the Old Law did not then, and does not now, apply to the Apostles doctrine for and in the church today.

The truth of the matter is made clear by Jesus. "When the disciples came, and said unto Him, "Why speakest thou unto them in parables"? He answered and said unto them, "Because it is given unto you to know the mysteries of the kingdom of heaven, but to them it is not given." (Matthew 13:10-16)

The difference and separation between the believers and the unbelievers is expressed even more strongly in Luke when Jesus said to his disciples, "Go your ways: behold, I send you forth as lambs among wolves." (Luke 10:3) The differences in the believers, the unbeliever, and the things spoken to each, are the same differences as in the meek, those who loved and honored him; and the rebellious, those who hated and murdered him. To attempt to put into practice those things taught to the unbelieving Pharisees (Note: Mathew 19:9), is to stand with them on judgment day.

Along with the differing people, the Lord was working in a time of great change. The arrival of Christ into the world, while preaching the coming of the kingdom, was certain to stir controversy as well as confusion. Much of that confusion remains until this day. The fear of placing total trust in Jesus is, yet, a topic of heated debate and strong disbelief.

Other than the believers and the unbelievers, there were the chosen and ordained twelve. Mark tells of Jesus, "and he goeth up into a mountain, and calleth unto him whom he would: and they came unto him, and he ordained twelve, that they should be with him, and that he might send them forth to preach". (Mark 3:14, Luke 6: 12-13)

The twelve Apostles were given instructions and insights which were given to no other people on earth. Jesus said to them in Matthew, "For verily I say unto you, that many prophets and righteous men have desired to see those things which ye hear, and have not heard them." (Matthew 13:17) Paul gives further testimony when he states, "Let a man so account of us, as of the ministers of Christ, and stewards of the mysteries of God." (I Corinthians 4:1)

The Hebrew writer gives insight concerning the preaching of the Apostles, beginning with the question, "How shall we escape, if we neglect so great salvation; which at the first began to be spoken by the Lord, and was confirmed unto us by them that heard him; God also bearing them witness, both with signs and wonders, and with different kinds of miracles, and gifts of the Holy Spirit, according to his own will?" (Hebrews 2:3)

In comparison to the overall amount of recorded teaching of Christ, the greater amount is directed to the Apostles. Much is given to the Apostles as a separate group that applies to no other individuals. John 13:31 through chapter 17 contains positive instruction given only to and about the office of the apostleship. The instructions include some basic principles, with the basic and practical application belonging only to the apostleship. This point clarifies much confusion when fully realized and cannot be over-emphasized.

In review, there are three separate and different groups of people, which are the believers, the unbelievers and the Apostles. Preconceived ideas concerning the teachings directed to the respective groups are the source of disagreement and divided beliefs among those believing in Christ Jesus as Lord and Saviour.

The book of Acts, following the first four books of Matthew, Mark, Luke and John, gives an account of some of the works of the Holy Spirit through the Apostles. Acts shows the beginning of the kingdom of Christ with the proclamation of the plan of salvation in the second chapter. The spread of the gospel message beginning in Jerusalem and over the known world is shown in Acts. The Apostle Paul speaks of his own efforts. " ...so that from Jerusalem, and round about unto Illyricum, I have fully preached the gospel of Christ. (Romans 15:19)

Acts is a written record that gives an easy plan to follow in the search for salvation. Instruction comes through examples and principles in addition to the direct commands of obedience to become a Christian. Acts is a unique part of God's word much like the books of Genesis and Exodus are exclusive in their positions. Each one marks a beginning. Each one introduces the new beginnings with miracles and signs. Each one sets down a plan for growth and continuance. The greatest difference in Genesis, Exodus and Acts is the time factor. There were no people to hinder the progress in Genesis. Everything was finished and set in motion in six days.

The book of Acts is followed with the letters of the Apostles and prophets written to churches and individuals. The epistles discuss further, the matters found in Acts. They give completion to the things spoken by the Lord concerning the church and the conditions to be met for salvation to become reality.

Christ had promised the Apostles, "These things have I spoken unto you, being yet present with you. But the Comforter, which is the Holy Spirit, whom the Father will send in my name, he shall teach you all things, and bring all things to your remembrance, whatsoever I have said unto you." (John 14:25)

During the same time period Jesus again said to them, "I have yet many things to say unto you, but ye cannot bear them now. Howbeit when he, the Spirit of truth, is come, he will guide you into all truth. These Scriptures show the proof of the coming event of the gospel in its completeness. (John 16:12)

The epistles are these things. "If any man think himself to be a prophet, or spiritual, let him acknowledge that the things that I write unto you are the commandments of the Lord." "According as his divine power hath given unto us all things that pertain unto life and godliness, through the knowledge of him that hath called us to glory and virtue: (I Corinthians 14:37, I Peter 1:3) Awareness of the specific instructions to the Apostles and their office is very important to a correct understanding of the over-all plan of the Bible.

Revelation is the last book in God's holy word. This book is very special in that it brings time and events to a close. It is an exciting and fearful book to read and think upon. There seems to be little agreement on many of the things shown. Yet there is a blessing promised those who read and understand. (Revelations 1:3)

Until this point there has been no notice given to the two sets of commandments found within each law for each time period. These are the moral and spiritual guidelines.

The moral law is the more easily recognized of the two. These are the things that guide us in our everyday association with family, neighbors, and co-workers in every aspect of our lives. Any correct human interaction demands attention to the moral laws which are given by the Author of everything good and right. As people draw away from God, the moral base shrinks in the maze of such things as ethics, expediency, and a general shift in moral values.

The spiritual laws are those laws which show us, as mortals, how to reverence our immortal God. Spiritual principles are easily missed or avoided, because in daily life, there seems to be no immediate consequence. We can go our merry way never aware anything is amiss. But God's will gives exact instruction in the matter of worship. Because these laws aren't spelled out in a "thou shalt, or thou shalt not" fashion, people worship the God of heaven any way they choose. People are confident that whatever their church doctrine calls for is all that is needed.

Faith and practice often rests on long standing church or religious traditions as the way to claim salvation. Still others depend on the human interpretation of specified, singular commandments and teachings of the Bible without diligently comparing the Scriptures to find the complete teaching for doctrine and practice. (I Corinthians 2:13)

We as mortals recognize moral wrong, social ignorance, political incorrectness, et cetera, but spiritual sin escapes our attention. This is true even in the face of numerous warnings throughout God's word.

"Brethren, my hearts desire and prayer to God for Israel is that they might be saved. For I bear them record that they have a zeal of God, but not according to knowledge. For they, being ignorant of God's righteousness, and going about to establish their own righteousness, have not submitted themselves unto the righteousness of God." (Romans 10:1-3) This is the exact and true substance in today's church scene.

"And for this cause God shall send them strong delusion, that they should believe a lie: That they all might be damned who believed not the truth, but had pleasure in unrighteousness." (II Thessalonians 2:10-12) It is ever so common for people to say, "It doesn't make any difference what you believe......," but read it again. The truth will become evident, remembering that error is multitude, and there are many, but truth is one, and stands alone.

"This know also, that in the last days perilous times shall come. For men shall be lovers of their own selves.....having a form of godliness, but denying the power thereof: from such turn away." (II Timothy 3:1-9) The Eternal Word of God is the power of God, for "by His word he brought the worlds into existence and by the same word they are reserved unto the day of judgment". (II Peter 3:5-7) Understanding the word of God, is the power of God unto salvation. (Romans 1:16) Where does this place the words of men that claim to preach another doctrine?

Throughout time, in every thing, God has provided men with all necessary elements for salvation. With the entrance of sin he has freely supplied direction in how to live among those around us, instruction for pardon of sin, and direction in how we may respect and show devotion to Him, as our heavenly Father. These things are listed in this order: "Now the end of the commandment is charity out of a pure heart, and of a good conscience, and of faith unfeigned." (I Timothy 1:5)

No stone is left unturned in providing man with every need and possibility for salvation.
"He that spared not his own Son, but delivered him up for us all, how shall he not with him also freely give us all things?" "If any of you lack wisdom, let him ask of God, that giveth to all men liberally, and upbraideth not; and it shall be given him.:" (Romans 8:32, James 1:5)

Everything is provided. These things are shown through commands and by examples from God in his dealings with people and events. The revelation of the written Word is presented in a manner that should not be considered difficult. It is indeed a practical arrangement.

For our time, within the Faith of Jesus, the Apostles are the example and pattern for anyone who will submit to God. The teachings of these men are an indisputable and inseparable part of the doctrine of Jesus Christ.

Recognizing the arrangement of the Bible eliminates much of the confusion commonly encountered when submitting our will to God. We can more readily know what is said to whom and why. Without recognizing the practical arrangement of God's Word, it is easy to become confused and discouraged. The requirements to be met in obtaining salvation are not difficult. Yet the Word always provides challenge for those who "hunger and thirst after righteousness."

CHAPTER TWO

SALVATION AND APOSTLESHIP ARE INSEPARABLE

Promises of Jesus Are Assured

All Promises of Jesus Are Not Directed To All People

Apostles' Position Must Be Respected

CHAPTER TWO

Salvation and the Apostleship are Inseparable

There are elements within God's word which requires faith but does not call for worship. Recognizing the place and power of the apostleship is one of the elements that is essential. The work and position of the apostleship is in the base and foundation of the kingdom of God. (I Corinthians 12:28) Respect is due the office without devotion to the individual persons involved.

In his tenure on the earth, most people see the work and life of Jesus very much in the same frame. There are things in his ministry that are more or less missed in the shuffle. One compelling point is that while on earth, Christ was occupied in three areas:
1. Fulfill the prophecies concerning himself.
2. Show himself as the promised Messiah.

3. Choose and prepare the twelve apostles to take the gospel to the world.

The appointment and mission of the twelve is a guiding factor in understanding the structure of the kingdom of Christ. Within the structure of the coming kingdom is the office of the Apostles. These men hold a unique place in the plan of God which no other Christian can claim. From the very beginning, before the foundation of the world, the promise of the Apostles was in God's plan. Ephesians 1:3-12 shows this to be true in every respect.

"Blessed be the God and Father of our Lord Jesus Christ, who hath blessed us with all spiritual blessings in heavenly places in Christ: according as he hath chosen us in him before the foundation of the world,...having made known unto us the mystery of his will, according to his good pleasure which he hath purposed in himself:...in whom also we have obtained an inheritance, being predestinated according to the purpose of him who worketh all things after the counsel of his own will: that we should be to the praise of his glory, who first trusted in Christ." The pronouns refer to the Apostles.

The pronouns must be given careful attention. There seems to be a common practice to assume that every Bible statement belongs to or is the responsibility of every Christian in general principle. This assumption cannot be true in so many instances; this is especially a false assumption in those things which Jesus gave exclusively to the twelve Apostles.

"For this cause I Paul, the prisoner of Jesus Christ for you Gentiles, If ye have heard of the dispensation of the grace of God which is given me to you-ward: how that by revelation he made known unto me the mystery;...which in other ages was not made known unto the sons of men, as it is now revealed unto his holy apostles and prophets by the Spirit;" (Ephesians 3:1-20)

Because the office of Apostleship was included in the sure word of prophecy, the Lord prepared himself with prayer in choosing the men he would qualify for the office.

"And it came to pass in those days, that he went out into a mountain to pray, and continued all night in prayer to God. And when it was day, he called unto him his disciples; and of them he chose twelve, whom also he named apostles." (Luke 6:12-13) The Lord in his appointment of the twelve did so with great concern for those whom His heavenly father would have him choose. To these chosen twelve, the Lord said,

"He that receiveth you receiveth me." (Matthew 10:40)

Luke goes further declaring,
"He that heareth you heareth me; and he that despiseth you despiseth me; and he that despiseth me despiseth him that sent me. (Luke 10:16)

Upon Peter's confession that, "thou are the Christ, the Son of the living God." (Matthew 16:16), Jesus told Peter,
"And I will give unto thee the keys of the kingdom of heaven: and whatsoever thou shalt bind on earth shall be bound in heaven: and whatsoever thou shalt loose on earth shall be loosed in heaven." (Matthew 16:19)

This was a specific promise to Peter. He would, through the Spirit, open the door to the kingdom, the church. On this, as well as other occasions, there were promises of law which were loosed and bound. All this happened as promised by Jesus throughout the four gospels and fulfilled in Acts 2.

The book of John tells of several promises made exclusively to the Apostles, which belonged to no other office or position. Beginning with John 13:31 and going through John 17 the Lord gave special instruction and prayer for this specific office. At this particular time, when these particular instructions were given, no one was present except the most faithful of the disciples. This means that on this momentous occasion, even Judas was excluded. None but the true and faithful were present. (John 13:30)

The Apostles are an undeniable part of the faith of Christ. Even though this is true, there are some points of Scripture in which some people feel there is a difference in the teachings of Christ and that of the Apostles. (Example: Matthew 28:19 and Acts 2:38 or Matthew 19:9 and Romans 7:2-3) Those who reason this way seem to think certain things said by the Lord are not said just that certain and exact way by the Apostles in any of their writings.

The implication is that of a possible difference in the teachings of Jesus and that of the Apostles, or that perhaps the Apostles left something out. With this line of reasoning, the words spoken by Jesus take precedence over that which is taught by the Apostles.

Any thought of these supposed differences in teachings should never be imagined, much less put into practice. This idea opens the door for major confusion as is now common in the present day church. When we, as mortals, find what appears to be a difference or missing link between Jesus and the Apostles' teachings, we have to know the fault lies in our own perception, not in God's Word.

"I have yet many things to say unto you, but ye cannot bear them now. Howbeit when he, the Spirit of truth, is come, he will guide you into all truth: for he shall not speak of himself; but whatsoever he shall hear, that shall he speak: and he will show you things to come. He shall glorify me: for he shall receive of mine, and shall show it unto you. All things that the Father hath are mine: therefore said I, that he shall take of mine, and shall show it unto you. (John 16:12-13)

Particular attention must be given in reading the instructions given to the Apostles. This is distinct and specific council to specific and exclusive people. These passages of Scripture should leave no doubt about the completeness of the doctrine of the Apostles. For that matter, this passage (John 16:15-16) should leave no doubt as to the incompleteness of the things taught to them up until this particular time. This is added to their inability to deal with what they were already taught before the coming of the Spirit.

Further the Lord said,

"Neither pray I for these alone, but for them also which shall believe on me through their word:" (John 17:20)

"Their word" is that which is found beginning in Acts and on through the letters of the Apostles and the prophets as they were led by the Spirit. This is now the sole source of faith and practice for those who will be faithful to God. (Galatians 1:6-9)

When reading instruction given to the exclusive benefactor, the casual reader may find difficulty in separating specifics from what appears to be general ideas. However, it is of the utmost importance to correctly understand what is given to whom and for what reason.

For their particular commission, the apostleship is defined as "select", and as separate as the king's princes whom he appoints over certain duties or provinces, or as the president with his cabinet members. The one who would presume to take the instructions of the president that he gives to his cabinet members would be presuming much without the proper credentials; this would constitute sedition. To bypass the written word of the ordained Apostles constitutes apostasy; in other words, the abandonment of the faith and doctrine of Jesus.

The Apostle Paul warns of this when he writes, "For such are false apostles, deceitful workers, transforming themselves into the apostles of Christ." (II Corinthians 11:13)

He also puts the matter forward in a very simple and pointed fashion.
"Now we command you, brethren, in the name of our Lord Jesus Christ, that ye withdraw yourselves from every brother that walketh disorderly, and not after the tradition which he received of us. For yourselves know how ye ought to follow us:...and if any man obey not our word by this epistle, note that man, and have no company with him, that he may be ashamed." (II Thessalonians 3:6-14) Again, note the pronouns and to whom they refer.

In addition to the message given to the apostles, he also reveals;
"Whereby, when ye read, ye may understand my knowledge in the mystery of Christ, which in other ages was not made known unto the sons of men, as it is now revealed unto his holy apostles and prophets by the Spirit;" (Ephesians 3:4-5) The importance of their authority must be acknowledged.

In a word, the Lord Jesus Christ is king of kings with his chosen, appointed princes. The laws and commandments taught by them are the binding commands from the Lord. To reach back beyond the appointed time and the appointed messengers, is to take as law and command the planning process which led up to the Lord taking command of his kingdom.

The commandments and exhortations to the Apostles in Matthew, Mark, Luke and John are part of the preparations for that which was to come in completeness. These things are that which lead up to the taking of office. After the office is secured, the laws of that office are proclaimed through the appointed officers; a matter of basic and common practice.
"Now then we are ambassadors for Christ, as though God did beseech you by us: we pray you in Christ's stead, be ye reconciled to God." (II Corinthians 5:20)

It may or may not be what we can take as personal instruction from the actual words of the Lord that will or will not save our soul; but it is correct to say that the things which the Lord gave to the Apostles is the binding factor.
"And when he had said this, he breathed on them, and said unto them, Receive ye the Holy Spirit: whosoever sins ye remit, they are remitted unto

them; and whosoever sins ye retain, they are retained." (John 20:22)

Jesus Christ is clearly giving an exact and definite plan of action for the expediting of the new law. This was to become a reality through none other than those appointed for the express purpose of preaching salvation to the world. These were the chosen of Christ, the twelve Apostles. (Acts 10:42)

The beginning church in Acts shows the path to be followed by future believers in Christ. Acts 2:42 makes it simple enough.

"And they continued steadfastly in the apostles' doctrine and fellowship, and breaking of bread, and in prayers."

If the Apostles' Doctrine was good enough for the first Christians, it should be good enough for Christians today.

"For I will not dare to speak of any of those things which Christ hath not wrought by me, to make the Gentiles obedient, by word and deed." (Romans 15:18)

The Apostle presents clear boundaries. The doctrine belongs to the Lord and Paul is the deliverer of that doctrine.

The Apostles' Doctrine is the substance and existence of the Commandments of Jesus. The doctrine of the Apostles brings in further instruction and insight in conjunction with those things shown in the four gospels. (John 14:26, 16:13) This does not give cause to imagine there are differences or contradictions in the testimony of either. Everything taught by Jesus and his apostles fit in complete agreement. In faith and doctrine they are one. (John 17:21)

There are no differences or blank places between the doctrine of Jesus and that of the chosen twelve. Since the period of the Lord's time with the Apostles on earth, there are only misunderstandings on the part of unlearned men, about what appears to be difference in the doctrines of each. In some instances these seeming differences are held almost universally among people of every known denomination.

But for every commandment of faith from the Lord Jesus, the correct understanding and application is in agreement with the letters of the Apostles and prophets. Recognizing the plan and order of the Bible and the part of the chosen Apostles solves otherwise unsolvable problems.

CHAPTER THREE

A SEAL OF THE RIGHTEOUSNESS OF FAITH

Jesus' Statements versus Current Popular Beliefs

The Scripture Needs No Interpretation

Jesus' and Apostle's Teachings Are One.

CHAPTER THREE

A SEAL OF THE RIGHTEOUSNESS OF FAITH

Simple facts of faith are often the most elusive. Much of the problem is caused by the availability of so many different religious doctrines. As a result, most individuals are intent on finding the group of people or doctrine that mirrors personal preferences.

The one part of faith which is most often wrapped in confusion involves baptism. Baptism is one subject that many religions do not take seriously until the time comes to join the church of choice. Then baptism in some form is required. The required baptism is not so much a matter of salvation as it is church group acceptance.

But the New Testament Law of Christ places great importance on the subject. Baptism is the end of past sin and the beginning of the new life. It is the being "born again" about which Jesus spoke to Nicodemus in John 3 and Paul clearly states in Romans 6.

Baptism is one part of the doctrine of Jesus that requires a material substance in its fulfillment. The substance is water. Immersion in water constitutes baptism as shown by an example in Acts 8:35-39, and other examples in Acts, as discussed throughout the New Testament letters. Baptism began to be taught with the ministry of John the Baptist, but it has a long history and a firm foundation throughout the Word of God.

Looking into the background of the subject of baptism, the catastrophic and the sublime are found in examples in past events. The flood that overwhelmed the earth in the life time of Noah can truly be called an example of the catastrophic baptism. As a baptism, the flood in Genesis, chapters seven and eight, has all the elements required, and performed all the necessary functions found connected with baptism. This baptism is given as a likeness to the baptism of Christ in the separation from past sins in I Peter 3:18-21. (v.20 R.S.V.)

The Flood of Noah's time divided the righteous from the wicked. It provided salvation for Noah from destruction with the world. This allowed Noah and his family the opportunity to live righteously in a world cleansed of its evil.

Baptism of great proportion is found again in the Old Testament in Exodus 12 when the children of Israel crossed the Red Sea. This baptism also fulfilled all the requirements of baptism. The Apostle Paul writes,
"Moreover, brethren, I would not that ye should be ignorant, how that all our fathers were under the cloud, and all passed through the sea; and were all baptized unto Moses in the cloud and in the sea;" (I Corinthians 10:1-2)

All the elements of separation and cleansing are present. The children of Israel were separated from the slavery and idolatry of Egypt. At the same time they were offered the freedom of true submission to, and worship of, the one God.

God performed these instances of baptism on a grand scale showing a pattern of separation from sin for those who would love their God and follow His commandments.

Baptism of the sublime nature, as a matter of faith in God, was introduced through the ministry of John the Baptist. Baptism was one of the important parts of preparing the way for the Lord's coming ministry.

From this point, people have created many ideas about baptism. Even among those of like beliefs, there are often differences of opinion as to the mode, pattern, and personal choice.

It is human nature for people to think they are in control of every aspect of their life, including eternal life. This is called *ignorant worship*. The Greeks in Acts 17:23 were warned about worshiping God ignorantly. The Jews were accused of "a zeal of God", but not according to knowledge, and being ignorant of the righteousness of God and going about to establish their own righteousness." (Romans 10:2-3) Ignorance on the subject of baptism is pervasive among those believing in Christ as Lord and Saviour.

The very beginning of faith in Jesus is clouded with doctrine from outside of revealed Word. For example, it is often stated that all one must do to be saved is, "believe in Jesus and accept him as your personal Saviour." The matter is correctly stated in John 1:12:
"But as many as received him, to them gave he **power to become** the sons of

God, even to them that believe on His name:"

The correct acceptance that is to concern the believer is that of whether the Father of Heaven *accepts us*. "Accepting Jesus as our personal Saviour" is based on the willingness to submit our will to him. Submission to His will is the key.

"Know ye not that to whom you yield yourselves servants to obey, his servants ye are to whom you obey; whether of sin unto death, or of obedience unto righteousness?" (Romans 6:16, John 8:34)

Baptism is one of the commandments of righteousness. Accepting baptism as a command is a giant leap of faith for some. Repentance and giving up old habits are also difficult human endeavors. Seeing ourselves for what we are in God's eyes is not an easy task.

We must not be ashamed to confess that Jesus is the Son of God. (Mathew 10:32) Confession of Jesus as the Son of God is as much a requirement for salvation as is faith. (Acts 10:9-10)

Every element in approaching the entrance into the family of God is a requirement. People want to discount one thing or another, but God's instruction does not say we can discount this or that at our convenience. Every commandment works in infinite perfection for a completed faith. Omission of any one thing destroys the wholeness of the plan of salvation. Any additional or deleted element only destroys the balance of perfection.

Baptism must be taken seriously. There is a cleansing that separates the believer from past sins and places him into the spiritual body of Christ. That cleansing is baptism. Without the element of water in baptism, there is no spiritual birth. Baptism into the death, burial, and resurrection of Jesus separates one from past sins and gives the privileges of fellowship in God's family. Romans, chapter six, shows the necessity of a change in conduct as a result of repentance and rebirth in baptism.

"Know ye not that so many of us as were baptized into Jesus Christ were baptized into his death? Therefore we are buried with him by baptism into death: that like as Christ was raised up from the dead by the glory of the Father, even so we also should walk in newness of life." (Romans 6: 3-4)

Baptism is not a matter of debate. It is a precise and careful part of God's will.

The importance of baptism is a mystery to most people who want to believe in Jesus. Many will even completely discount baptism. As created creatures, people do not realize that the choices are not theirs. The only choice is to accept or reject the commandments of God.

Each individual belongs to Christ.
"For ye are bought with a price". (I Corinthians 6:20)

Baptism is the vehicle or means that places one into Christ and makes one a part of the body of Christ.
"For you are all the children of God by faith in Christ Jesus. For as many of you as have been baptized into Christ have put on Christ." (Galatians 3:26-27) Baptism is the part of the birth process that places one into the family of God through Jesus Christ.

Outside the family of God there is no benefit promised. Life as a Christian begins when baptism is accomplished. The gift of the Holy Spirit is then given as an earnest of our inheritance. (Acts 2:38, Ephesians 1:13-14) In avoiding or rejecting the commandment of baptism, the accomplishment of full faith and acceptance of Jesus as Christ is impossible.

The definition of baptism, from the Bible perspective, gives the correct understanding and usage of the term of baptism as a **commandment of the Lord**.

In its most simple definition, baptism is an immersion, a covering up, a submersion, a burial in water. (Mark 1:10, Acts 8:38-39, Romans 6:3-5) The element in baptism is water. Water is the cleansing and separating element. Jesus informed Nicodemus,
"Verily, verily, (or, truly, truly) I say unto thee, Except a man be born of **water and of the Spirit**, he **cannot** enter into the kingdom of God." (John 3:3-5) The re-birth of our spirit begins with faith and repentance upon learning the truth.
"Faith comes by hearing and hearing by the word of God." (Romans 10:17)

The process of re-birth brings about confession of Christ as God's son with submission to the commandment of baptism. Baptism requires water as part of being born again.

The Jews and the disciples of John did not seem to have any trouble understanding the purpose of baptism in John 3:25.
"Then there arose a question between some of John's disciples and the Jews about **purifying**. And they came unto

John, and said unto him, Rabbi, he that was with thee beyond Jordan, to whom thou barest witness, behold, the same **baptizeth**, and all men come to him." (John 3:25-26)

Parties on both sides of the question understood that baptism was a purifying of sinful men. Baptism and purifying are synonymous.

Paul speaks of the purpose of baptism and its significance;
"...and gave himself for it (the church): that he might sanctify and cleanse it with the **washing** of water by the word," (Ephesians 5:26)
"...according to his mercy he saved us, by the **washing** of regeneration, and renewing of the Holy Spirit;" (Titus 3:5)

The commandment of baptism is that washing which was commanded of Saul of Tarsus. Ananias came to him and said,
"And now why do you delay? arise, and ***be baptized, and wash away thy sins***, calling on the name of the Lord." (Acts 22:16)
Ananias did not tell Saul to call on the name of the Father, and of the Son, and of the Holy Spirit.

Baptism by faith is "the washing of regeneration." Note the phrase, "with the washing of water by the word." The Word of God sanctifies the water. The water fulfills the requirement of the Word, satisfying the need for regeneration and the renewing of the Holy Spirit, according to His (God's) revealed Word.

Every element contained in the commandments of God works together in an unbroken chain. Men are not authorized to change or ignore any one thing. One who chooses to discount any one or any number of the commandments of the faith causes the faith to become null and void for that individual.

Baptism in water, is the commandment for salvation which relates to "having our bodies washed in pure water." Without it, the evil conscience continues to be ours.

When the spiritual birth is compared to the natural birth, recognition of the close likeness is interesting. Without a generous supply of moisture, the physical birth is impossible. Water in varying forms is an absolute necessity to the physical birth process. Whether the human heart wants to believe it or not, water is a necessary element in the spiritual birth.

Without spiritual birth, the promised strength and force of the Spirit is allowed to break in continuity. With that break in the spiritual continuity, death comes to the flow of life that comes through the power of the Word of the Spirit.

"For whosoever shall keep the whole law, yet offend in one point is guilty of all." (James 2:10)

Adding to or detracting from the necessary element, at the very point of birth, is disastrous.

" ...but ye are **washed**, but ye are sanctified, but ye are justified in the name of the Lord Jesus and by the Spirit of our God." (I Corinthians 6:11)

If one is not **washed** he is not sanctified, (set apart). If one is not sanctified, he is not justified. Without justification there is no salvation. Everything in the faith and doctrine connects and cannot be broken without leaving salvation unfulfilled.

"...let us draw near with a true heart in full assurance of faith, having our hearts sprinkled from an evil conscience, and our bodies washed with pure water." (Hebrews 10:22)

The power to become the sons of God comes through the commandment of the One whom God sent to save a sinful world from sin. Note carefully the phrase, "to them gave he power to **become** the sons of God." Following closely the order and context of John 1:12 shows that faith in Jesus and the confession of His name gives believers the power and privilege, or right to go on to **become** sons of God. Accepting that right in baptism is the choice. The only choice.

Jesus himself settled for nothing less than the perfect will of God. With submission of himself to baptism, Jesus was revealed as the beloved Son of God to the world. With our own submission to baptism we are also recognized as children of God.
"For ye are all the children of God by faith in Christ Jesus. For as many of you as have been baptized into Christ have put on Christ." (Galatians 3:26-27)

This one thing expresses the compelling significance of baptism. We are either in or out of Christ. Baptism is the placement factor.

The commandment of baptism is an innate part of salvation. People who are knowledgeable of the faith of Jesus can appreciate this fact. However, there is a problem for some people in what appears to be a difference of command as given by Jesus in Matthew 28:19 and that given by the Apostle Peter in Acts 2:38, in addition to examples shown throughout Acts and the epistles.

The reference in Matthew reads:

"Go ye therefore, and teach all nations, baptizing them in the name of the Father, and of the Son, and of the Holy Spirit."

The passage of Acts 2:38 reads:

"Repent, and be baptized every one of you in the name of Jesus for the remission of sins, and ye shall receive the gift of the Holy Spirit."

Considering these two passages side by side (Matthew 28:19 and Acts 2:38) the attention is focused on the number of names in relation to the baptism. Considering these two passages in and of themselves, there seems to be differences which cannot be reconciled through the Scripture. This is due to the phrasing in Matthew 28:19 not being found again in connection with baptism. As a result, likenesses of the two passages fade significantly.

For some, there seems to be a conflict with Matthew commanding baptism in the names of three; the Father, the Son, and the Holy Spirit, while Acts teaches baptism in the name of one, which is Jesus. Matthew 28:19 is seen as a command being spoken and commanded by the Lord Jesus, who is divine. This is different and preferred over that which was commanded by Peter, who is a man and not the Christ. Thus, admitted or not, it is deemed as closer to correct and necessary to prefer the command of Jesus over the command of Peter.

The first consideration concerns the reference term "name" and the individuals to which the name relates. The terms used in this verse, (Matthew 28:19), show reference to individuals only, without any names given. Second, when the singular term "name" is used in other references, the name of Jesus is given or is in direct reference to Him, so why are there apparently three names mentioned in this reference? Third, what is the purpose of baptism? Standing alone, this passage answers none of these questions.

The final concern is the "name" or "names" in which baptism is commanded. The singular form of the term "name" is used in both references. People interpret the term "name" in Matthew 28:19 as a plural term. Acts 2:38 gives the singular use of the term "name", referring to the one Jesus, given for salvation to become ours. (Acts 4:10-12)

Matthew 28:19 is composed of simple words which are used often in everyday speaking and writing. For this reason people feel comfortable with what the passage appears to be saying. Because of the familiar words used in this passage, it seems to be the very essence of simplicity. Yet, what appears to be basic and simple matters, are often more difficult to bring to an understandable explanation.

With this in mind, Scripture to support the commonly held understanding of Matthew 28:19 is needed. Questions need answers concerning what this passage is saying, how it corresponds with, and is in harmony with the remainder of teachings about baptism.

In the search for related references, interesting points become apparent. A pattern emerges for the phrase, "in the name of" because the term "name" is consistently in the singular form. The same phrasing is found in the reading of Matthew 28:19 and Acts 2:38 and others.

Outside the reference Scripture, there are no supporting Scriptures upholding the popular belief and usage surrounding Matthew 28:19. The conclusions drawn are dependent on pure human understanding of this verse. Jesus had not yet ascended and the Spirit had not yet been sent to the Apostles. At this point, there is no explanation and Bible students accept Matthew 28:19 as law with no further questions entertained or answers acknowledged. This Scripture has been applied erroneously. People are being baptized in the name of the "Three" versus in the name of the "One" due to their lack of faith in the "One Saviour".

Most believers in the faith of Christ understand that the Father, the Son and the Holy Spirit, as shown in Matthew 28:19 are designated personalities. But knowledge of exactly who they are is gained from other places in the written word. In using Matthew 28:19 as a singular text, very little can be known about any part of the subject matter. If this one passage will stand alone on this one point, it would be an exception.

The problem is to discover the actual content of this passage beginning with whom the baptism is in relation to, and to whom the "name" belongs. (Baptism is related to this term no matter to whom it applies). What, then, is the position of each one, and how do they relate to each other in the matter of baptism? Matthew 28:19 in and of itself answers none of these questions.

The "name" is the one which is honored in baptism. This name is related to the three in the Godhead. (Colossians 2:9) The three are the Father, the Son and the Holy Spirit. In comparing Matthew 28:19 with other passages of

Scripture, the names of the three are supplied, along with how each relates to the other.

To realize the greater understanding of the essential elements and how they work together, the word "of" is a word that demands attention and definition. There is no useful purpose in avoiding or lightly regarding this term with its position and power in this reference. In finding a synonymous term for the word "of", the content of Matthew 28:19 is more easily comprehended.

As a result, the phrase "in the name of", with the correct understanding in relation to the connective "of", will come to have a meaning that is in keeping with the doctrine and principles that relate to baptism.

When the phrase "in the name of" is shown to be, "in the name pertaining to", the usage and understanding of Matthew 28:19 become quite clear. This "name", the "name of Jesus" does pertain to the three in the Godhead.

"Go ye therefore, and teach all nations, baptizing them in the name **pertaining to** the Father, and **pertaining to** the Son, and **pertaining to** the Holy Spirit."

What is the name that pertains to, or is of the three, but the name that is above every name, the name of the Lord Jesus Christ. The name, Jesus, is "of" the Father because the Father gave this name to the only begotten Son. (Matthew 1:21) The name is "of" the Son because this is the name by which he was called. (Matthew 1:25, Luke 2:21) The name, Jesus, is "of" or pertains to the Holy Spirit because the Spirit revealed this name. (Luke 2:26)

This understanding is compatible and in keeping with the design and objective of the message in the Scripture as a whole. The purity and intent of the message is left unaffected and unbroken with every part working together to complete the whole of God's Word.

The message in the passage of Scripture found in Matthew 28:19, as well as any other passage that appears to be a one time quote does not stand alone. There are distinct and separate parts within the whole of God's Word. Nevertheless, every part supports every other part to complete the perfect will of the Father.

The same pattern follows through for the working relation of the three in heaven. This harmony and simplicity is demonstrated in Matthew 28:19. The same harmony is found in I John 5:7-8.

These three are separate personalities with separate positions, each with an active and powerful part in the plan of salvation. Yet none of the three of heaven work separately or alone, but in a harmony which is perfect and undivided. Exactly how this is accomplished is often difficult to bring to a simple point of recognition.

Most believers of the Lord Jesus have no trouble with the reality of the existence also of the Father and Holy Spirit. Knowledge of this existence comes about as a result of Scripture reference to their appearances at the same time on several occasions.

An example of their appearance in one place is at the time that Jesus was baptized of John. (Matthew 3:13-170) Another example is the mount of transfiguration. (Matthew 17) However, any real bringing together of the Scripture in explaining the position and part carried out by each, does not seem to be a topic of general perception. When a simple layout of the working relationship is stated as follows, it all becomes quite clear.
            God is the father of all,
            Including Christ.

I Cor. 3:21-23

Christ is the mediator of all,
Including God.
Gal. 3:20, I Tim. 2:5

The Holy Spirit is the messenger of all, including man.
Rom. 8:26-27, Eph. 2:18

GOD, CHRIST, HOLY SPIRIT
Three in Person
Three in Position
Three in Work
One in Purpose

The things of the Spirit are an endless guessing game to the human mind. Even those things which are not difficult are viewed as that which must be obscure or complicated to be correct. Therefore, when a simple matter is explained in detail, to the point where there can be no misunderstanding of the passage content, there arises every objection and excuse imaginable to avoid the obvious truth. Within almost any current modern day church which practices baptism this is the course of action.

Regardless of various beliefs, Matthew 28:19 is in agreement with the Apostles doctrine of baptism in every respect. There are not any choices to be made on the part of mortal man to choose between the commandment of Jesus and that of His chosen ministers, the Apostles.

The importance of the position of Christ the mediator is full and comprehensive. It includes any and everything that exists between God and man or man and God. Entrance into the family of God begins with Jesus and ends with Jesus, including baptism in His name.
"For ye are all the children of God by faith in Christ Jesus. For as many of you as have been baptized into Christ have put on Christ". (Galatians 3:26-27)

Regarding the position of the Apostles, Paul writes,
"For we preach not ourselves, but Christ Jesus the Lord; and ourselves your servants for Jesus' sake. For God, who commanded the light to shine out of darkness, hath shined in our hearts, to give the light of the knowledge of the glory of God in the face of Jesus Christ. But we have this treasure in earthen vessels, that the excellence of the power may be of God, and not of us:" (II Corinthians 4:6-7) Those earthen vessels are the Apostles.

The faith and baptism that is believed and practiced must be that one that is taught by those whom Jesus appointed to deliver the gospel to the world. This must be done regardless of what we may want to think of those things which Jesus taught to those who were appointed and ordained as His messengers to the world. We must not become guilty of the apostasy of avoiding the commands given to those appointed to bring salvation to the world.

"Therefore if any man be in Christ, he is a new creature: old things are passed away; behold, all things are become new. And all things are of God, who hath reconciled us to himself by Jesus Christ, and hath given to **us** the ministry of reconciliation; to wit, that God was in Christ, reconciling the world unto himself, not imputing their trespasses unto them; and hath committed unto **us** the word of reconciliation. Now then **we** are ambassadors for Christ, as though God did beseech you by **us; we pray you in Christ's stead,** be ye reconciled to God." (II Corinthians 5:20)
This passage is assurance that the Apostles taught the gospel message in every sense.

The whole of the written word of God is complete and perfect, needing no outside interpretation.
"Knowing this first, that no prophecy of the Scripture is of any private interpretation." (II Peter 1: 21)

The Written Word is fully self explanatory. Matthew 28:19 is a part of Scripture and therefore not subject to the interpretation of men. In comparing the passage with Acts 2:38, along with other related passages, the likeness and agreement of the two passages is established.

Because this is so, the question is this; when was the change brought about that instituted baptism in the names of the three in the Godhead?

This is answered from the volume called, the Catholic Catechism, a Contemporary Catechism of the Teachings of the Catholic Church, written by John A. Hardon, to quote:

*"The Didache (Composed before A.D. 80) told the faithful what they must (and must not) do. (Page 334) The sacrament of baptism is conferred by infusion (pouring) or aspersion (sprinkling) of water or by immersion in water while the one who baptizes pronounces the words, "I baptize you in the name of the Father and of the Son and of the Holy Spirit. When the Second Vatican Council treated the sacrament of baptism in its various documents, it carefully distinguished between the **unchangeable** faith of which the sacrament is the visible expression,*

*and certain **ritual changes to be made in its administration.*** (emphasis added).

*"We know from the gospels that baptism was conferred by water and words, where the words pronounced were those recorded by St. Matthew, i.e., "in the name of the Father, and of the Son, and of the Holy Spirit." The Trinitarian formula is specified in the first century Didache, which indicated that at least by the year A.D. 100 this was the common usage, **whatever may be said about baptizing "in the name of the Lord Jesus"** as recorded in the Acts of the Apostles.* (p. 511), (emphasis added).

How brazen! How daring! (Compare I Timothy 4:1-3, Revelation 2:20-23, 17:1-18, 18:1-24)

Some of these apostate teachers doubtless were those on whom the Apostles had laid hands in the giving of the gifts of the Sprit. This gave them gifts and powers, and thus influence, that they soon assumed they could use to draw away followers to themselves, as Paul had warned they would in Acts, chapter 20.

The doctrine that teaches the Trinitarian formula of baptism comes to the religious world straight from an apostate doctrine. There are few exceptions among those who profess to believe in Jesus that do not use this doctrine and form of baptism. This is regardless of the purpose or mode of baptism practiced by each individual group.

While speaking to the elders of the church in Ephesus, Paul warned them to
"Take heed therefore unto yourselves, and to all the flock, over the which the Holy Ghost hath made you overseers, to feed the church of God, which he hath purchased with his own blood. For I know this, that after my departing shall grievous wolves enter in among you, not sparing the flock. Also of your own selves shall men arise, speaking perverse things, to draw away disciples after them." (Acts 20:28-30)

According to the very words of those who brought in the perverse things, the changes were not long in arriving. They were firmly implanted long before the close of the first century. Remember, the Apostle John wrote the book of Revelation before the close of the first century. He warned and rebuked the churches about the false teachers already at work.

The Apostle's command is baptism in the name of the Lord Jesus through the word of the Lord Jesus, as revealed to them by the Spirit sent from the Lord Jesus, as promised by the Lord Jesus.

The Trinitarian formula is from the minds of men and not from the Lord Jesus Christ or his ordained Apostles.

Everything that is received from God comes by, in, and through Jesus and in his name. Jesus said, "And whatsoever ye shall ask in my name, that will I do, that the Father may be glorified in the Son." Baptism for the remission of sins is the first thing we ask in the name of our Lord after confessing our faith in him as the Son of God. Baptism is the petition for, and an appeal to God for the forgiveness of sins through the resurrection of Jesus.

Again, "Baptism which corresponds to this, **now saves you**, not as a removal of dirt from the body but an **appeal to God** for a clear conscience, **through the resurrection of Jesus Christ.** (emphasis added) (I Peter 3:21, R.S.V., ASV)

It is possible to take all the correct steps for the right reasons, and then take a sharp right or left turn before entrance is made across the threshold to salvation. This is what is accomplished with faith in Jesus, repentance of sin, confession of faith in Jesus as the son of God, and ending with the universally recognized Trinitarian form of baptism.

Privilege is granted to everyone to believe and practice any baptism in any name and any doctrine that is desired through the Trinitarian baptism. However, the promise of God rests in baptism in the name of the Lord Jesus Christ as shown through the Apostles.

Anything that appears as an element of contrast or disagreement between Matthew 28:19 and Acts 2:38 comes only from the minds of men who, without a complete and humble study of the Word, will follow their own personal understanding.

Galilee is where Matthew 28:19 issued forth. Salvation did not come out of Galilee. The obtaining of salvation began to be taught first in Jerusalem. This was firmly promised in the last words of Jesus on the earth. "And that repentance and forgiveness of sin should be preached to all nations beginning from Jerusalem. (Luke 24:47)

The Apostle Paul said, "And of your own selves (the elders of the present time) shall men arise"...then the warnings from the Lord through John in Revelation 2:6,15 about a strange name and a strange, undefined doctrine. The Apostle

Paul warned the Ephesian church. Turning to Revelation the same church at Ephesus is commended for hating the doctrine of the Nicolaitanes. The Church of Pergamos was condemned for allowing those within the Church of Pergamos to hold to that doctrine.

I Corinthians 1:11-13 shows the church becoming factious, calling themselves by names belonging to men. Who is the man named Nicolas in Revelation 2 who was drawing away disciples into an apostate doctrine? Those people, on whom the Apostles laid hands and gave the miraculous powers, surely were equipped to lead people astray. Leading astray the unaware and unstudied was the most opportune place to begin a sphere of influence. The resulting agenda teaches them the "very words of Christ" in one single statement. This neglected the witness and corroboration of the complete doctrine; then the entrance of an ever widening variety of doctrines can be introduced at will. We must be aware that all we ever hope to gain in Christ must come through the doctrine as presented by the Apostles.

II Timothy 2:5 warns that Christians are instructed to be on constant alert to Satan's devices. This calls for daily study and daily prayer. (II Timothy 2:15)

Every worthwhile effort in this life carries with it specific rules, instructions, and guidelines. These are necessary to achieve a correct and effective result.

There is the same requirement for eternal salvation to be ours. So very many spiritual minded people who want to trust God also want to believe He will let us slide by on this or that point. There are no promises on this act of carelessness.

CHAPTER FOUR

HEBREWS: THE UNIQUE EPISTLE

Central Purpose of the Book of Hebrews

Acceptance of Change in the Law

Gospel Revealed To Hebrew Writer by Witnesses

CHAPTER FOUR

HEBREWS: THE UNIQUE EPISTLE

The book of Hebrews comes to us in a little different manner than the majority of letters written to Christians and the church in general. It is an important writing with distinct elements brought together. With these elements brought together, the central purpose is served perfectly. The book of Hebrews leaves nothing to supposition.

The first chapter announces the intent and purpose of Hebrews. This is to show to Jewish Christians, Jesus as the indisputable Son of God and Savior of men apart from the law of Moses. Yet, he is shown through and by the very law, to which the Jewish nation claimed to maintain a strong loyalty.

The proof of Christ and his doctrine is offered through the prophecies and with the fulfilling of them in His life, death and resurrection. The perfection and superiority of the law of Christ over the Law of Moses is shown in the book of Hebrews by parallels in several areas of the Old Law.

The Old Law is shown to be the shadow and figure of the New Law which follows it. "For Christ is not entered into the holy places made with hands, which are the figures of the true; but into heaven itself, now to appear in the presence of God for us:" (Hebrews 9:24)

In writing the book of Hebrews, the writer brought together and set in order, information already available. This was done while examining and explaining the connection and meaning as he moved on with the central theme. While following that central theme, facts of evidence are brought together in an orderly fashion. Everything is assembled in a manner that is forceful, yet one of simplicity.

In a powerful and direct manner, the writer shows the deity of the Lord Jesus as the Christ through use of the law and prophets. This was the Law from which the Jewish Christians couldn't quite free themselves. There was difficulty in comprehending the fulfillment of prophecies before their very eyes.

The Jewish that were Christian at that time, are as many people of today: they could not convince themselves that the law and all it implied for the Jewish nation, was no longer effective.

"For there is verily a disannulling of the commandment going before for the weakness and unprofitableness thereof. For the law made nothing perfect, but the bringing in of a better hope did; by the which we draw nigh unto God." (Hebrews 7:18-19)

It is safe to say there are no hidden mysteries newly revealed in the Hebrew letter as is so often found in the writings of the Apostles, Peter or Paul. (I Corinthians 15:51, I Peter 1:10) The information discussed in the book of Hebrews is found elsewhere in the revealed Word of God.

The book of Hebrews fulfills a unique mission. The fulfilling of this mission is accomplished without directly naming the Apostles or their office by name. In this New Testament book the author isn't revealed even though many

Bible students strongly believe the Apostle Paul to be the author. The assumption is based on material found in chapter 5:11-14 chapters 12, and 13, along with other possible references. These references contain several statements which sound familiar. Frequently it is thought to sound like this or that writer.

Some, who feel that Paul is the writer, will do so with the qualifying statement, "If Paul be the writer". The qualifying statement will usually follow some pertinent quote from the book of Hebrews. This isn't a definite claim because a definite reference of proof is not available.

Even so, anyone who would hint that Paul possibly may not be the writer, is given to understand that to do so is a mistake because the idea cannot be proven from scripture. Nevertheless there are occasions when "who isn't" can be proven without finding "who is".

The book of Hebrews does not give direct information about the singular personal identity of the author. There are passages that reveal who is not the writer or writers. These passages, when held in comparison to those passages which show how Paul received his knowledge in the gospel, leave an unmistakable message. The message is that none of the Apostles should be considered as writers of the Hebrew letter.

The first passage for thought reads: "How shall we escape, if we neglect so great salvation; which at the first began to be spoken by the Lord, and **was confirmed unto us by them that heard Him?** God also bearing them witness, both with signs and wonders, and with divers miracles, and gifts of the Holy Spirit, according to his own will." (Hebrews 2:3-4)

This passage is often read with emphasis upon the first half of verse three. But with close examination, another important element comes to light. The important element is that the writer of the book of Hebrews lists himself among those that had the gospel confirmed unto them by someone other than the Lord himself. Also note Hebrews 4:2. "For unto us was the gospel preached, as well as unto them".

It is important to understand that the writings of the Apostles show the message revealed to them to be revealed directly through the Spirit. It was not because of hearing the message through preaching. Paul leaves no doubt when writing in (Galatians 1:11-17).

"But I certify you, brethren, that the gospel which was preached of me is not after man. For I neither received it of man, neither was I taught it, but by the revelation of Jesus Christ.. .But when it pleased God, who separated me from my mother's womb, and called me by his grace, to reveal his son in me, that I might preach him among the heathen; immediately I conferred not with flesh and blood: neither went I up to Jerusalem to them which were apostles before me;"

In sharp contrast to statements from the Hebrew writer, the Apostle Paul gives the clear, unmistakable message as to how he received the gospel. The Apostle Peter also gives clear and open understanding in how all the apostles received the Word.

"Unto whom it was revealed, that not unto themselves, but unto us they did minister the things, which are now reported unto you by them that have preached the gospel unto you with the Holy Ghost sent down from heaven: (I Peter 1:12)

"For we have not followed cunningly devised fables, when we made known unto you the power and coming of our Lord Jesus Christ, but were eye witnesses of his majesty." (II Peter 1:16)

In examining this point, the letters from Paul, Peter, John or Luke, the personal pronouns "I" and "we" are used. Until the last few verses of the epistle, the Hebrew writer, or writers, also use the terms "we" and "us" in making personal references. Some examples are, ". . .we have many things to say. .. ", "Now the sum of the things which we have spoken. .." (Hebrews 5:11, 8:1). It seems therefore, entirely possible that the book of Hebrews was written by more than one writer.

Of the thirteen letters of the New Testament that Paul is credited with writing, every one of these letters began with the name of Paul. The first word penned is the name Paul;

"Paul, a servant of Jesus Christ",

"Paul, called to be an apostle of Jesus Christ".

This is the heading at the beginning of each and every letter authored by Paul. The Apostle Paul himself gives witness to the fact of his personal signature in each letter he writes.

"the salutation by the hand of me Paul."

"The salutation of Paul with mine own hand, which is the token in every epistle: so I write. "(I Corinthians 16:21, Colossians 4:18, II Thessalonians 3:17)

The evidence of authorship is undeniable in each letter written by Paul. There is not the slightest amount of real evidence about the person of the author to be found in the book of Hebrews. The book of Hebrews is opened with a completely different format than is used at any time by Paul.

Hebrews is written primarily to show the lordship of Christ. He is the focal point. His authorship of the New Law, and its superiority over the Law of Moses, is the topic under discussion. This is so strongly shown throughout the whole of the book of Hebrews, until any kind of distraction from this purpose seems to be avoided. The important mission of the book nullifies the introduction of any other issues.

The Apostles consistently held the position of being preachers and teachers of others. Paul and the other apostles are shown to have received the message of the gospel by direct revelation from the Lord. There is no doubt the Hebrew writer wrote with inspirational guidance with the basic knowledge of the gospel being received from "those that heard Him"

The interest in the authorship of Hebrews gives no input into the matters under discussion. But, when people feel there is something they wish to know, they will also feel free to engage in supposition. Nevertheless, statements by the Apostle Paul and things shown throughout this letter, show that he is definitely not the writer.

If it were necessary or important for the person of the writer or writers to be known, it would have been revealed. In matters pertaining to salvation, believers of Christ Jesus know there are no blank spaces in the plan of salvation for late day minds to fill.

Yet we often find that where people think there is no damage done to the continuity of the total elements involved, they then feel they are not treading dangerously or infringing on forbidden ground when engaging in some small supposition. This happens often in every day life. Human nature is so comfortable with this type of activity until it is second nature to carry it straight into the church. The subversion of the written Word of the Almighty is the end result.

The Hebrew writer warns of the willful sin.

"For if we sin willfully after that we have received the knowledge of the truth, there remaineth no more sacrifice for sins,...It is a fearful thing to fall into the hands of the living God." (Hebrews 10:26–31)

Paul warned against those that would alter the revelations shown through his writings. The same warning is sounded for all of God's word.

"And if any man obey not our word by this epistle, note that man, and have no company with him." (II Thessalonians 3:14)

The book of Hebrews is a book all its own. It sets the plan and pattern down in an order that shows the basic structure of the complete revealed Word from beginning to end. Additional information concerning the possible author would add nothing useful or inspirational to the message.

The reason or purpose for supposition on the part of the human element is invalid and unprofitable. The book of Hebrews is a valuable part of the will of the Father in heaven and none should dare to tamper with the teaching found there. But people often do not hesitate, voicing opinions and adding a little thing or two when they feel there is a possible lack in some point. And too, there are some who may feel the subject of authorship is unimportant. We, as created creatures, are not the judges in these things. Everything that is written in God's Word is to be held in reverence.

For who hath known the mind of the Lord that he may instruct him?" (I Corinthians 2:16)

"He that is faithful in that which is least is faithful also in much: and he that is unjust in the least is unjust also in much." (Luke 16:10)

Religious teachers are very adept at a little change here or there. One little thing at a time leads to vast and sweeping changes over the long term. (Galatians 1:6-9) Anointing Paul as the author of Hebrews is an anointing from man. This is one seemingly insignificant change with monumental implications.

CHAPTER FIVE

First a Wife. . . . Or a Christian?

Infractions of Christ's Spirit of Law and Letter of Law

God Created the Office and the Occupant

"Different" Misconstrued as Better or Worse

CHAPTER FIVE

FIRST A WIFE ... OR A CHRISTIAN?

Subjects discussed up to this point are concerned with certain passages of Scripture in an examination of the letter of the law. The use or misuse of these passages affects the spirit of the law in accordance with the usage. The next subject is primarily a matter of the spirit of the law. Misuse of the spirit of the law leads to infractions of the letter of the law.

Within the usual realms of home, church, and society, any earnest discussion of male-female relations stirs strong emotions, and natural prejudices come sharply into focus. Emotions become even stronger in the area of husband and wife relations. When emotions are in control, opinions and natural human thinking will hold sway, regardless of compelling Bible principles.

Because of a lack of study in these matters, many of the truths are not recognized. Even if these truths are realized, deliberate ignorance sets in. Obvious details and plain facts concerning Scripture as well as human nature are refused, and even held in contempt.

Evidence in the Word of God shows that man and woman were created in a different way and time sequence than were the creatures of the animal kingdom. Genesis 2 shows detail and order that is taken lightly and brushed aside.

It is written, "that man was created out of the dust of the earth. (Genesis 2:7) God then breathed into his nostrils the breathe of life, and the man was alone. After the man was created several events took place. Each act of God was for the benefit of the human race and served an important purpose.

The first event was to prepare a place for man. God planted the garden eastward in Eden, where he then placed the man. (Genesis 2:8) While Adam was yet alone, he was given the moral principal of physical labor. (Genesis

2:15)   Then the spiritual principal of reverence for God was introduced with the commandment concerning all fruits that were to be freely eaten, including the tree of life. (Genesis 2:16)   The one exception was the tree of knowledge of good and evil. (Genesis 2:17)

"And the Lord God said, It is not good that the man should be alone; I will make him a help meet for him. And out of the ground the Lord God formed every beast of the field; and every fowl of the air; and brought them unto Adam to see what he would call them; and whatsoever Adam called every living creature, that was the name thereof. . . . but for Adam there was not found a help meet for him. (Genesis 2: 18-20)

The responsibilities of keeping the garden, obeying the command not to eat of the tree of knowledge, the task of giving names to the animals, were Adam's while he was yet alone.

The creation of woman is unique in that after everything else was finished, she was then created. She came on the scene as no other creature on earth in that she was created from a principal part taken from the man, and not directly from the dust of the earth. The creation of woman, stands apart as the crowning glory and finishing touch of all that God created. Eve was presented to Adam as a gift. (Genesis 2:22) The gift cost him nothing of any great consequence. She was his without any planning or labor on his part. Human nature usually becomes careless with that which cost them nothing or for which they did not labor. He quickly neglected the greater role of stewardship in the family unit.

It is without dispute that from the beginning the man was given the responsibility of leadership. The woman was given the supporting role as the 'help meet'.

Quote, "And the Lord God said, it is not good that the man should be alone; I will make him a help meet (suitable) for him." (Genesis 2:18)

In many ways and in many areas men have taken this one idea and expanded it to mean that he was given the right of placing responsibility where he will, without accepting the consequences for his own actions. Example: "And the man said, The woman whom thou gavest to be with me she gave me of the tree, and I did eat."

At the time Eve was presented to Adam, he made the commitment of responsibility that he was soon to ignore. Also at this time Adam had not yet made the decision to eat from the tree of life. He chose instead, to delay this all important opportunity. This and other acts of delay led to disaster for the human race. The occurrence of the first sin, is the most grievously sorrowful event in the history of the human race. The flow of events gives witness to Adam's casual disregard for godly instruction. But, the first overt transgression was not the first act of carelessness and neglect.

The culmination of events in the garden began when the serpent appears and converses with the woman. The events that followed have important pivotal points that have remained with the human race throughout time. For the majority of people, the chief point of interest is the statement that God made to Eve, ". . .and thy desire shall be to thy husband, and he shall rule over thee." Out of this statement, authority over the woman is thought to be law and command to the man.

Many religious sects, groups, etc., suggests Eve is subjective to mindless, mandatory obedience. "Thy desire shall be to thy husband..." Actually the statement has inexpressible wonder and profound meaning. What woman, especially the Christian, does not truly desire close companionship and oneness of thought and spirit with the man she marries? The purpose in marriage for the Christian, is companionship free of outside intrusion, close in likeness to the skin and the body. (Think of the skin as it protects and covers, how it tingles or chills as the body rejoices or suffers.)

"and they shall be one flesh." (Genesis 2:24)

In truth, it is a statement about the organization of things already in place. "For Adam was first formed, and then Eve." (I Timothy 2:13) But the statement in Genesis 4:16 also has a double edge for Eve. It tells her on the one hand that she will seek to please and placate, while he continues his neglect with a sense of justification

In the natural human scheme, the process of courtship presents the very obvious idea of a lifetime of mutual caring and companionship. Generally speaking, the outcome of the scenario shows that she marries for joy and happiness; he marries to control. She marries expecting freedom of communication and closeness of thought and life in general. He marries feeling that he has conquered and acquired a possession over which he can now rule. She marries for emotional and spiritual intimacy and he marries for status and public image. She hopefully marries a sweetheart and love of her life, only to find a judge with a double standard. While she seeks to be one in heart and soul, he construes this as her bid for control over him. The abiding concern for any ruler is to maintain power.

Each personality is its own. Human effort to re-mold another person's spirit and mind will wreak havoc in the life of another and create the unexpected and undesired result.

So what are the implications of one ruling over another? What are the responsibilities, rights, and privileges of one that is head over another? What are the responsibilities, rights and privileges of one that has another over them? Both positions are accompanied with these things.

Customary events show the rights and privileges belonging to the ruler, while the accountability belongs to the one being ruled. Whether on a personal or social level, this proves to be the end result.

Many problems come about because of deeply seated ideas in how wives, and women in general, are to be treated by the men and society in general. Because of deeply seated ideas, many human concepts are brought directly into the religious situation without question or second glance. This can be said as surely for the thinking of the women as for the thinking of the men. There are common ideas shared by both. Because these ideas are shared, they are regarded as undeniable and righteous. Any attempt to test these concepts in light of Scripture, is harshly frowned upon. A study of the number of areas in which accepted norms contradict God's word of instruction would reveal a shocking truth.

In religious circles, the more closely people consider themselves to be strictly Bible believing, the more the authority of the men over the women is stressed. As men are taught leadership, the more the subservience of women is emphasized as mandatory and not to be questioned. In stressing the authority of the men, the wives are expected to conform to the expectations of their husbands in every area of life.

The prevailing attitude about the feminine office in the Christian realm is demonstrated in an article written by Raymond E. Harris dated July, 1988. At that time he was the minister for a church group in Sheffield, Alabama. According to Mr. Harris there are four (4) areas of reconciliation which are taught in the New Testament. His list includes, "Brother to Brother", "Wife to Husband", "Jew and Gentile", and "Man to God". In discussing the reconciliation of "Brother to Brother", Mr. Harris says, and I quote:

> "It should be noted that this is the only passage (Matthew 5:24) in the New Testament using a term denoting MUTUAL hostility and MUTUAL concession. In other words, in such a dispute the innocent party has nothing to repent of and need not make concessions. Only the guilty must adjust his course of action!"

The second subject of reconciliation listed by Mr. Harris is, "Wife to Husband". Of this reconciliation, Mr. Harris says:

> "In I Corinthians 7:11, Paul explains that a woman who departs from her husband (when he has not committed adultery) has but two choices. She must

remain unmarried or "BE RECONCILED" to her husband. The word "reconciled" in that passage is used as a verb denoting action. The very nature of the term here indicates that the woman having departed, must make the concession or adjustment and return to her husband".

The attitude and spirit displayed in this article concerning the wife, is one which is frequently shown among those considering themselves strict Bible conscious people. Mr. Harris seems to feel that adultery is the one and only sin a man can commit against his wife.

The above statements from Mr. Harris are remarkable in their content and attitude. They are remarkable because none of us are without sin. In almost any adult dispute, it can scarcely be said that one party is guilty of all the wrongs while the other has contributed nothing to the entanglement.

The sins of fear, ignorance, pride, and neglect are the plagues of the race as surely as the sins of deliberate commission. The problems of life demand mutual recognition, repentance, and reconciliation.

Because of emphasis upon doctrines of Scripture concerning wives, the position of husband and wife are often discussed with the view that each position is at odds with the other. Almost any instruction to wives about their position in the church and home is taught as a contrast, rather than complimentary, to the position of the husbands.

The quotes from Ephesians 5:22, Colossians 3:10, and I Peter 3:1 are quoted regularly. These passages include the statements which read, "Wives submit yourselves unto your own husbands, as unto the Lord". These passages are used forcefully in any massage delivered which relates to women and their position in the home and church.

At times there may be a smile or some light wit, but the message is there, declared often, and to the point. As a whole, men take it upon themselves to seriously expound and resound upon these direct and explicit instructions to women. This is usually done with an attitude which is lacking in any genuine display of charity, kindliness, or equity.

The belief that the wife is first a wife and then a Christian is evidenced to the point of being the accepted standard. Without making the direct statement, the message is that the wife must obey the husband and trust his guidance, for her Christian faith to be a valid faith.

Within this framework are strong indications that the men have no confidence in their wives, and feel they must constantly be "kept in line" in every area. Also, there is the suggestive inference presented that the feminine gender is unable to maintain faith in Christ without male intervention. I Peter 3:7 is quoted regularly with the emphasis placed upon the phrase, "the weaker vessel". Because it is supposed that women are weaker, any problems that arise in the marriage is then credited to the feminine part of the relationship.

Yet, for all their supposed weaknesses, it is feared by the male gender that women will take over at the slightest provocation. So what is the solution? How are Christian women to navigate such a contradictory situation?

The Christian woman, with any serious knowledge of God's Word, doesn't seek the leadership role designated to the man in the family structure. Within the family structure the Christian husband and wife are given appointed positions that are closely related. For one to forcefully interfere with the other is to violate his own.

Nevertheless, questionable pressure is stressed heavily without due consideration for the sensitive feminine nature. These matters are preached with no special reference given to times, places, events or individuals in relation to the message preached. Women, because they are women, are wrapped in a package and labeled. This is especially true when the subject is submission to the husband.

The point of view put forth from more than one pulpit says, "women are to be in subjection to men". I Corinthians 14:34-35 and I Timothy 2:11-14 are the key passages used to support this premise. The passages read:

"Let your women keep silence in the churches: to be under obedience, as also saith the law. And if they will learn anything, let them ask their husbands at home; for it is a shame for women to speak in the church." (I Corinthians 14:34-35)

"Let the woman learn in silence with all subjection. But I suffer not a woman to teach, nor to usurp authority over the man, but be in silence." (I Timothy 2:11-14)

One lady relates the experience of a fellow becoming overly zealous with the idea of masculine control. The particular point of discussion was fornication. The fellow was in the throes of seduction toward the lady, his belief being that this act could be justified in some circumstances. As the final argument, he heatedly insisted with the idea that "According to Scripture", women are to be in subjection to the men."

This man was a church minister and supposedly a man of God, seeking to mislead a new convert by saying that when one is deeply spiritual, physical acts do not matter. It illustrates how Scripture will be twisted in instances of the misinformed and/or the unawareness of some, when there is purpose and intent on the part of another. This also serves to prove that the spiritual life cannot be reflected from a corrupt moral setting.

The Apostle Paul said,

"But I would have you know, that the head of every man is Christ; and the head of the woman is the man, and head of Christ is God." (I Corinthians 11:3)

The Lord Jesus Christ is the head over every man; but it is certain, every man is **not** the head over **every** woman.

Furthermore, the Lord God never requires the unqualified submission of one mortal to another. Examination of the elements involved in I Corinthians 14:34-35, I Timothy 2:11-14 will show the position of women, married or unmarried to be for the duration of assembled worship.

Women are to maintain a passive behavior in keeping silence, not assuming leadership during congregational worship. This behavior is as the written Word commands throughout time for the godly woman. (I Peter 3:5) Women are given a place and purpose in the worship to God. The place and purpose is participation.

This demonstrates the contradiction when women are often reminded that "their place" is not that of leadership. Yet the men give full permission, when placing women in the leading teaching positions which involve children. This holds true in or out of the Christian religions where children are present, except the Church sporting events. Then the men shine. But the male habit of neglecting their duty to their children follows them right into the church teaching situation.

Leadership and teaching positions come in varying degrees and differing areas of Christian living. One office isn't qualified, adapted, or capable of satisfying all things for all positions. Note should be given to this when studying the passages surrounding Acts 6:2-4. The Apostles instructed the multitude (men and women) to choose those who would oversee the ministry to the needy saints. "and the saying pleased the **whole** multitude," (Acts 6:5) For the same reasons, there is more than one position of leadership in the home.

Regardless of this truth, most individuals who are in leadership positions in the Church presume the position of leadership results in the right to unconditional authority for some, with unconditional submission for others. The supposed unconditional authority isn't to be questioned by those who occupy supposed less notable positions.

Acceptable submission would require the wife to entertain no desires, needs, or even spiritual aspirations beyond those maintained or permitted for her by her husband. Added to this, she is expected to understand these boundaries by virtue of becoming a wife.

The commandments to women "to be under obedience", "to learn in silence with all subjection", "not to usurp authority over the man", is quite appealing to the basic human nature. Caution should be the word because these things are very easily distorted and used for personal pride with a justified sense of self righteous control.

It has been said that sin is never committed with so much glee as when done in the name of God. Misapplication of the commandments to women are surely in such a category.

In considering the psychological and emotional differences between men and women, the matter of submission to the husband is not the difficulty for the Christian woman that some people are determined to suppose. This would be easily realized if the wife were given the honor commanded and due her for the role and responsibility which is hers by appointment from God. In so many religious situations, the responsibilities of the husband to his wife are scarcely noticed when compared to the amount of attention given to teachings for the position of the wife.

The teaching for the Christian woman about her submission is emphasized in sermons preached, classes taught, and materials published. According to the comprehensive theme, the single most important element in the Christian woman's faith is obedience, with the obedience to her husband being the one important element above any other aspect of Christian living.

This type of situation contributes heavily to the problem addressed by the Apostle Paul.

"Husbands, love your wives, and be not bitter against them." (Colossians 3:19)

Assuming from the attitude displayed in the afore quoted excerpts from Mr. Harris, and from many sermons preached, there is much bitterness toward wives. Bitterness is a valid problem in the marriage relation, as shown in the fact that the Apostle Paul has directly addressed the problem. When due respect is not present, bitterness creeps in and feels justified.

Much of the bitterness and doubt arises because the lusty nature of men utilizes that same lusty nature as the standard in placing judgment on their wives. There is the natural tendency of the one over the other to measure by personal weaknesses. Appearances of truth are assumed in this placing of judgment due to sermon themes being without reference to particular acts, instances, or individuals. These things are taught from the pulpit to women, whether married or single, about their place in life, as a matter of urgent necessity.

This strongly suggests that married happiness is an empty hope. That which was created to satisfy good and righteous purposes, is judged suspect simply because certain Christians (women) are thought of as less important or in a lower position by comparison.

In any study of the principals of doctrine and the office of women, there are women in the Lord's church who are unwilling to submit to God's will. When the occasion arises, it should be duly noted. Corrections should be immediate and take place in relation to the particular individual, time, and circumstances.

It is difficult for anyone, whether male or female, to explore the subject of wives and their role in life, in an unbiased manner. Some of the difficulty arises because of the need for a tough and honest, self examination regarding personal motives.

Few are the church or social leaders that can logically examine the realistic importance of the place of women in God's creation. Added to this, people in teaching positions are not as dedicated to the examination of their own inward selves as they are in examining the intention and actions of those they consider to be lesser. As a result this area of Scripture isn't given careful study for passage content and meaning.

There are separate and easily understood passages written directly to wives and women as a separate and collective group. In regard to these passages most men do not see, and women are blind, to the fact that God has given specific instruction to Christian women. It applies to women only and is apart from those things which apply to men, children, or strangers among the congregation.

This instruction applies to women only in their position as women and more specifically as wives. It should be noted; it is not given expressly to men to be passed along to the women. According to scripture, women are to teach women in matters that pertain exclusively to women. (Titus 2:4-5)

It is regrettable that the manner in which these Scriptures are used serves only to further the natural arrogance and conceit of the husband, and men as a whole, toward wives and women as a whole.

In this matter also, the truth of the scripture is abundantly appropriate. The Scripture reminds us,

"But the natural man receiveth not the things of the Spirit of God: for they are foolishness unto him: neither can he know them, because they are spiritually discerned."(I Corinthians 2:14) The majority of religious men have no comprehension of the spiritual doctrine of Jesus in relation to family.

Most assuredly, matters concerning women are to be taught. Nevertheless, in teaching that which governs the position or office of another, extreme care must be exercised. In teaching things which belong to another's line of duty, one is not to assume the personal obligation to enforce obedience and compliance in accord with personal demands. Among religious groups seeing themselves as strict or fundamental believers, it is firmly accepted that the husband has the right to keep his wife in subjection to his (the husband's) rules of conduct. Heavy burdens are placed upon others when people feel that their place in life justifies their demands.

There is a point, often quickly read but never emphasized, in the reading of the passages directed to wives. The unemphasized lesson is that these passages are addressed directly to wives. They are directed to the wives with the expectation that the wives are able to read, comprehend, and act accordingly. The quote reads, "Wives submit **yourselves...**". It is found in Ephesians 5:22, Colossians 3:18, and I Peter 3:1 with slight variations in wording. These passages are directed to women. This needs to be recognized for what it is saying, and to whom it is speaking, in order for a balanced view of the Scriptures to prevail.

Because the commandments are directly to wives, the decision to obey is one which belongs to the wives. For the husband to assume he is to force, coerce, or malign his wife into subjection is to commit a gross misapplication of the law of Christ. Again, the command reads: "Wives submit **yourselves....**" Neither the command nor the principle is found that commands the man to bring his wife into submission.

There is no doubt that our Heavenly Father recognizes the nature of humanity when it feels or experiences power over another, for any reason, real or imagined. This awareness is shown in I Peter 2:18-25 followed by 3:1 and other commandments to wives, and also servants. As a result, women (and servants) are given precise guidelines to cling to and hold in times of stress.

With the greater percentage of women, there is the desire to please their husbands. This is the natural and normal design of the Creator. As it is written, "...and thy desire shall be unto thy husband'. (Genesis 3:16) Among Christian women, the percentages are greater and the desire is stronger. She is more aware, because of her position as a child of God.

In observing the commandments to women, and wives in particular, the older women are to teach the younger women. "The aged women likewise, that they be in behavior as becometh holiness that they may teach the young women to be sober, to love their husbands, to love their children, to be discreet, chaste, keepers at home, good, obedient to their own husbands, that the word of God be not blasphemed." (Titus 2:3-5)

These three short verses cover a large area in the daily existence of Christian women and the relationships they may encounter. This is instruction on a large scale, yet is instruction directly to women. Thus we find the primary instructors to women, in matters pertaining to women, are other women; the older women.

Few are the men who are able to understand, with genuine concern, the nature of the feminine gender. This doesn't change for the Christian, by virtue of obeying the Gospel of Christ. The persistent lack of quality discernment and comprehension of the wife gives indication of this fact. As a result, statements made by the wife are often doubted and held as suspect.

There are physical, psychological, and emotional differences in the inherent nature of male and female. For either one to understand the other, much is required in patience, sincerity, and persistence, as well as tough personal honesty. Because of these differences the older women are the only qualified teachers for younger women. Young people do not understand many things about life and its entrapments. The older, truly Christian woman is well equipped to guide the younger in matters of knowledge, patience, and endurance in connection with the Christian life.

As a general rule, the masculine gender does not recognize this principal as a part of the word of God. Because of the differences in male and female discernment and evaluation systems, men do not recognize the feminine intellect as having truly useful value.

Human nature when given authority has the tendency to assume that what is correct for their own personal needs and desires is also correct for others. It has the tendency to assume that "different" is defined as more or less, better or worse. This is true more than ever for the one in authority over another. For the husband over the wife, the assumption is made that his standards are correct standards for her. He assumes this is all she needs, all that is necessary for her best interest. All too often women are classified as less, therefore less deserving in material, spiritual and emotional areas. It seems to be second nature to understand different, to mean less worthy.

Christ offers his mercy to us in an earnest, caring, and unbiased manner. This offer contains all the promise, purpose, and protection for every situation, for both the husband and his wife.

"I am come that they might have life, and that they might have it more abundantly." (John 10:10) Husbands seem to feel it is their duty to place limits on this abundance for their wives. The wives react as though this promise is not theirs to claim. As difficult as it may be to comprehend, every promise the Lord gives to Christians, includes Christian women.

The Lord never forced his will upon us. He offers and then leaves the decision to each individual. But this isn't the way the majority of Christian husbands behave toward their wives. It is forgotten that in actual fact the wife is as much the free-will agent with the husband as the church is to Jesus. Submission must be free, not forced.

Leaving the problem of submission to those responsible for the submission would remove tension from many situations. The husband could be released of useless worry and mistrust. Men as head over their wives, seem to expect the submission and reverence from their wives that they themselves refuse their Lord and Saviour, who is the head over them!

If Christian men could free themselves from this anxiety they would then be free to be the example of the obedient follower of Christ. This would leave the wife free to be the help meet for which she was created. She would not be forced instead, to deal with often inflicted hurts and frustrations. Many times, these are the direct result of the husband imposing his will on the wife for useless reasons.

"Ye shall know the truth, and the truth shall make you free", not put you in prison. (John 8:32)

The natural consequence of enforcing obedience often involves keeping tabs on each and every action of the wife. Thus begins the making of demands for compliance. Often the demands are without useful purpose, or are totally foolish in nature. One of the things Jesus taught in the Lord's prayer is not considered;

"And lead us not into temptation." (Matthew 6:13)

"Let us not therefore judge one another any more: but judge this rather, that no man put a stumbling block or an occasion to fall in his brother's (fellow Christian) way." (Romans 14:13)

"For ye are all the children of God by faith in Christ Jesus. For as many of you as have been baptized into Christ have put on Christ. There is neither Jew nor Greek, there is neither bond or free, there is neither male nor female; for ye are all one in Christ Jesus." (Galatians 5:26-27) Add to this, "That God is no respecter of persons." and it becomes a weighty matter indeed. (Acts 10:34)

"Young men likewise exhort to be sober minded, in all things showing thyself a pattern of good works: in doctrine showing uncorruptness, gravity, sincerity, sound speech that cannot be condemned."(Titus 2:6-8).

The quote from Titus is graphic instruction to young men. Instruction in matters of male/female relations is sorely lacking in most structured religions. Young men, who are young in maturity, or young in the Faith, do not come by the above attributes as a matter of natural course. The natural course allows him to feel he is appointed and superior, from the beginning; that God just naturally prefers him to any female.

Young men must be taught these qualities. These are the things which will sustain a man as well as his family. The instructions given to men and women in this particular reference relate closely to each other.

The exhortations to both men and women are given in a solemn manner. There are no qualifying statements in either set of instructions. It is serious, to the point, instructions for each.

Adam said: "This is now bone of my bones, and flesh of my flesh: she shall be called Woman, because she was taken out of man." (Genesis 2:23)

Strengths and weaknesses in both male and female can be seen with close examination of the text. The woman was taken from the man and must of necessity inherit some of the weaknesses.

"For as the woman is of the man, even so is the man also by the woman; but all things of God."(I Corinthians 11:12)

Women, whether Christian or not, are presumed to be weaker in spirit as well as in body. Statements are often made indicating that any woman is more likely to sin whereas the man, being stronger, is less likely to commit the same sin in any given situation.

The other side of the coin will show the way strength and weakness can be used. The stronger chooses to use his strength to take a risk, whereas the weaker would fear to engage in the same activity. One, who is weaker and also recognizes his weakness and vulnerability, would abstain.

Men, especially religious men, display the attitude of thinking themselves strong and in control of their fleshly desires. At the same time, indications are shown as to their own personal ideas about the inability of Christian women to maintain personal integrity. Thus women are judged weak and apt to be carried away in doubtful situations solely by virtue of their feminine nature.

Then because of their supposed strength, men seem to think themselves able to participate in various marginal or dubious areas without fear of permanent marks or possible damage to body, mind, or soul. The more strength one feels for himself, the more allowances he will make, and the more risks he will take. Weakness as well as strength can be used for salvation or for destruction.

Lest we forget, as surely as woman came from man, the term "weaker" derives from the term "weak". In other words, women may be the weaker vessel, but this does not nullify the fact that men are weak. Women are usually weaker than men in physical terms. In recognizing their physical weakness they are often more aware and careful. Those of the human race who consider themselves strong and/or able will seek to hide weaknesses and often set out to prove themselves to the world. Whether male or female, each have their weaknesses. Both are mortal.

"Likewise, ye husbands, dwell with them according to knowledge; (knowledge of, or in what? What else but the knowledge of God's word on the subject) giving honor (Honor!!) unto the wife as unto the weaker vessel.. ." (I Peter 3:7)

The term "weaker" is used in several recognized versions. The correct term would be "sensitive". The terms used in Webster's dictionary to define "weak" are negative to the last word. Is this the realistic view of the feminine gender from the beginning? Didn't God say "I will make him (Adam) an help meet"?

In physical strength and endurance, men are stronger than women. Being physically weaker is no offense in God's law. The larger part of the problem in dealing with I Peter 3:7 lies in the fact that the woman is referred to as the weaker vessel. It is as though something of less value, less moral, or less spiritual is implied to the minds of most people. Many strong impressions are left along the way in the usual discussion of this subject matter. It is as though the term "weak" defines all aspects of the feminine nature.

By design, men are in the positions of rule and authority. This is easy to accept in moving from a child into adulthood. Additionally we have the male instinct that feels superior to the feminine gender solely by virtue of physical strength and gender.

On the opposite side of the coin, Christian women are usually under some form of accountability throughout their life. They are in submission to someone, in many areas of life, for one reason or another. The correct reason would be for protection for the physically weaker of the two.

But many people want to assume so much more from this and as a result, problems are created. The feminine gender thus is placed in the position of the exploited. This does not end upon accepting a religious faith. All too often it will increase. Pride and physical strength remain in control. However,

"Many that are first shall be last, and they that are last shall be first." "For whosoever exalteth himself shall be abased; and he that humbleth himself shall be exalted." (Luke 13:30, 14:11, I Corinthians 1:27)

Despite the opinion displayed by many Christian husbands, the position of the wife is appointed and ordained by the Creator. The position has its own responsibilities. It is a position that women are capable and fitted to fulfill. The one that will presume to mind the office of another corrupts the end result of that appointed office.

Falling short of his own duty, the individual becomes a busy body in the affairs of another. (II Thessalonians 3:10-14) I Peter 4:15 lists the meddler on equal footing with the murderer, thief, and the evil doer. Men and women each have a place in life. Each has a work to fulfill. Neither one is to "think more highly of himself than he ought.' (I Corinthians 4:6-7)

The place, office, position, ministry, of women in the home, church, and society in general is unique and distinct in many respects. Anyone that will discount the feminine position and responsibility hasn't considered the Source (God) of the plan.

"For as we have many members in one body, and all members have not the same office: so being many, are one body in Christ, and everyone members one of another." (Romans 12:3–8) Galatians 3:27 also applies here. Therefore, no single Christian member is to held above the other, for every member functions in conjunction with every other member. As Christian memembers are parallel to members of our body, each one must be given due respect.

I Corinthians 3:16 is to be seriously considered when thinking of the misuse some people heap upon their own bodies because their head decided commit some indecent act.

"Know ye not that ye are the temple of God, and that the Spirit of God dwelleth in you?" "If any man defile the temple of God, him shall God destroy; for the temple of God is holy, which temple ye are." "So ought men to love their wives as their own bodies. He that loveth his wife loveth himself. For no man ever yet hated his own flesh; but nourisheth and cherisheth it, even as the Lord the church:" (Ephesians 5:28-29) "This a great mystery but I speak concerning Christ and the church". (Ephesians 5:32)

Then consider the possible defilement of the one, while causing no bodily suffering or emotional strain to him who has the power over another. The damage can be beyond calculation.

"Having then gifts differing according to the grace that is given to us.. ." (Romans 12:3-13) "Now there are diversities of gifts but the same Spirit..." (I Corinthians 12:4-28)

The heavenly father created both male and female. Each were given some of the attributes of God himself, some different and some the same for both.

"But as God hath distributed to every man, as the Lord hath called every person, so let him walk." (I Corinthians 7:17)

Christians, whether male or female are included in the admonition. There are gifts and abilities which differ between the two. Submissiveness is one trait or gift all its own. May it be said that submission for most women is much easier to accomplish than for most men. Let it also be noted that the individuals that are likely to have the least control over their own selves are the ones who seek to control others.

Because most men are not of a submissive nature, they seem to assume that same nature is not to be found in the woman they marry. This creates problems which threaten the survival of any marriage. Many problems arise from a lack of respect for the fellow Christian to whom one is wedded. One Christian cannot place temptation or force upon another and consider himself "head of the wife, as Christ is the head of the church". Obedience to God, for each individual, must be gained of one's own free will. Were these principles taught in their true context and God's plan for male and female recognized, the dominating nature would be deprived the sanctimonious joy of inflicting his own standards on those whom he considers less creditable.

If, in reality, the wife were under only her own husband, the hardship would possibly, not be so great. But that is hardly the way it happens. This is evidenced by the undeniable fact that men will keep account with each other to see that each one keeps the pressure on. One of the ways this is accomplished is through suggestive remarks and mocking accusations. This particular type of behavior is the accepted standard and it gets results. Consequently, the wife is truly under the burden of many, instead of only one.

The submission of the wife is in *her* control. There are those who will dispute this, but read further.

"Wives, submit yourselves unto your own husbands, as it is fit in the Lord."(Colossians 3:18)

Submission of the wife to the husband is measured according to the standards found within God's word for submission. How many are the men that will lead a wife into immoral acts to test for compliance with his demands.

"Therefore as the church is subject unto Christ, so let the wives be to their own husbands in everything." Many religious people take the position that the last two words of this reading are the binding factor. "Let the wives be subject unto their own husbands in everything." A powerful statement. But "everything" in what area? The husband who does not submit to Jesus Christ in everything is not qualified to demand or accept the Christian's submission. He does not possess correct standards of behavior even for himself, much less for another.

These few verses and like readings found elsewhere in the Scriptures, are the prime sources of lessons taught to women regarding her position in church, home, and society. These passages are made to sound as though the wife has no higher calling than to submit to her husband's every demand, justified or not.

What is the answer to such a dilemma? "Wives, submit yourselves unto your own husbands, (note) as it is fit in the Lord." (Colossians 3:18) Important point: The wife is duty bound to practice **selective** obedience. There are limits in submitting to any mortal, including one's husband. But in preaching and teaching situations, the last phrase of Colossians 3:18 is handled as almost none existent. Exaggerated over emphasis of some points of Scripture to the neglect of others is a convenient tool for those who will use the will of God for personal gain and to further their own ideas.

Christians are warned, "Dearly beloved, I beseech you as strangers and pilgrims, abstain from fleshly lusts, not using your liberty for a cloak of maliciousness, but as the servants of God." This warning will apply anywhere, including the family. (I Peter 2:11-16)

Every Christian wife is required to exercise discretion in obedience to any who might seek to exert authority. No Christian, whether male or female, is ever required to yield in total and blind obedience to any other mortal.

Each individual Christian has the obligation to search out truth and reject error wherever and from whomever it may issue forth. For one mortal to depend upon another mortal for eternal life, is unthinkable.

It does not matter how long a thing has been believed or practiced when it is in error. Many ideas and attitudes of long duration are put forth in matters of feminine submission that are far removed from the truth.

Regardless of long held ideas, women have a certain amount of responsibility for their own salvation. The first allegiance of any individual is to the Lord Jesus. If this is allowed its righteous course, submission to one's husband will be more correctly accomplished. Women are not exempt from personal liability by reason of submission to sinful requirements of a sinful husband.

Witness the threat of hypocrisy entering the infant church in Acts 5. A man named Annias and Sapphira, his wife, had agreed to sell property. They claimed they were giving the total proceeds to the support of those in need in the early church at Jerusalem. As the matter progressed she was given opportunity to separate herself from the plan, but chose to continue the deception. For this she paid the same penalty as her husband.

However, the husband does have a vested interest in the matter of the salvation of his wife.

"But I would have you know, that the head of every man is Christ; and the head of the woman is the man; and the head of Christ is God." "For the husband is the head of the wife, even as Christ is the head of the church:" (I Corinthians 11:3, Ephesians 5:22,31 & 32)

The elements involved gives the man a position of influence and notable degree of control. The fact that the husband is the head of the wife, gives him a greater degree of responsibility for the welfare of his wife. But because of the human weakness for total control, the husband must be careful. James wrote,

"My brethren, be not many masters (teachers), knowing that we shall receive the greater condemnation." (James 3:1)

Christ Jesus is head of the body, the church. (Colossians 1:18) As the head he leads and guides. Because the husband is the head of the wife as Christ is head of the church, he is in the position of teacher and leader of his wife (if he is a devoted child of God) as the Lord Jesus is teacher and leader of the church.

It is written,

"And Adam was not deceived, but the woman being deceived was in the transgression." (I Timothy 2:14)

There is an interesting point in this reference. Eve was deceived, and ate. Nothing is said of Adam being deceived, but he ate anyway. Yet most people seem to believe Eve was totally at fault and alone in the first sin.

Within most religious bodies this incident is discussed in Bible classes. The repeated attitude is as though the woman was guilty not only of her transgression, but was guilty for his sin also. There isn't the severity displayed for Adam's part in the transgression as is exhibited in the discussion of Eve's transgression.

Eve was first in the transgression of God's only command of a negative nature, namely, "Thou shalt not...". Incidentally, this commandment was given to Adam, even before Eve was created. (Genesis 2:16-17, 21) There is a general understanding that there was only one commandment that was in force in the garden. The one thing was, to not eat of the forbidden fruit. Yet Adam did not maintain his own commitment to cleave unto his wife. Because of Adam's lack of commitment, Eve faced the tempter without any assistance from her husband.

Upon first reading the passage beginning with Genesis 3:1 it sounds as if Eve were alone in her meeting with the serpent. Nothing is said of the presence of Adam until verse 6 when "...she took of the fruit thereof, and did eat, and gave also unto her husband with her and he did eat." Close examination of Genesis 3:6 shows Eve was not alone in the meeting with the serpent. Adam was there observing everything. Apparently he made no effort except to take and eat.

When Adam is questioned concerning his part in the transgression he makes his defense. "The woman whom thou gavest to be with me, she gave me of the tree, and I did eat." Eve was not alone in her sin. Adam, being totally aware of all events, said nothing. Silence can be golden, at times. Then again it can be cowardly consent. After the deed was done, Adam then attempted to make himself appear the innocent victim by laying the blame at the feet of his wife after first blaming his God.

Adam did not cleave to his wife in this matter by offering assistance to overcome the temptation. When it came time to give account, he did what most normal men do. As with Adam then, so it is now. The male is, for the most part, afraid to admit or confess any guilt or weakness without first pointing to the female as the cause of his wrong doing.

Job makes a statement about the sin of Adam in his plea for understanding.

"If I covered my transgressions as Adam, by hiding mine iniquity in my bosom:" (Job 31:33) Blaming another for personal transgressions lets no one out, including the first man to try it.

With most fundamental groups, much is read into the necessity of the obedience of the wife. Yet, one point isn't brought forward nearly so forcefully or clearly, and that is the matter of the burden of leadership.

To be the head, or a leader of others, makes one accountable for the nurturing and care of those over whom he is head. In the transgression in the Garden of Eden, Adam did not accept his share of responsibility either before, during, or after Satan's bid. Therefore God gave him the position of the responsibility which he had tried so fervently to avoid. But men think this has given them the right to be judge and jury over everything the wife says and does.

None of this is to encourage wives to disregard an overbearing husband. There is the sure admonition to the wife in I Peter 2:18 continuing through chapter 3. These and other admonitions give comfort and guidance. The guidance serves well for the times when the way becomes confusing and hard to bear.

Neither is this to hint that the wife is not to be in submission. What is being questioned is the proposition of one child of God enforcing his own religious ideas on another.

The Christian wife is to be in submission to her Christian husband. But let us remember whose decision it is to accomplish this submission. She is to do this according to her ability. It is often humanly impossible to satisfy the demands of others. The husband isn't the power and force in the matter of submission. Assist? Yes. Set demands to be met and coerce into submission? No!

So often there is the human tendency to deal with the wife's part in marriage as a separate entity that isn't influenced by other commandments for Christian living. Not only is this true in respect to matters between husband and wife but also in comparison to other Christians.

The general attitude is exhibited that the feminine marriage partner is not deserving of the same consideration as other members of God's family, especially when family problems arise. Partiality and respecting of persons isn't a matter of concern. Within the marriage relation, in matters of righteousness and sin, kindness and harshness, justice and injustice, more is expected from the wife in the way of tolerance for her husband than she is to expect in return from him or other Christians. The double standard is present among those professing faith in Christ, as it surely is in the world at large. The feminine part of the relation is the first to be held up to scrutiny in times of family trouble.

The attitudes and actions of various ministers and teachers often show a separate aspect of self-righteous judgment toward wives which isn't shown to any other category of believers. The problem is magnified in times of family crisis. It is normal procedure for the wife and mother to receive the brunt of criticism. Because these attitudes and actions may be in relation to women, or the wife specifically, does not prove them to be justified.

In the marriage relation, as with any other area of life, time is given to choose between good and evil. The choices which come, and the way the application of these choices are conducted, will prove the undoing of those who think nothing of placing responsibility where none is due.

This is possibly true in the husband and wife relation more than with any other. The reason for this is because of the daily opportunities available for offense. It is easy for anyone to victimize that which is taken for granted because it is thought to be warranted by virtue of the position as head over another.

Ephesians 5:22-23 is taught and fervently adhered to by many of the believers of Christ. But it is with an attitude of exacting authority over the wife. It is no less necessary for the other side of the instruction to be taught to bring balance into the family life of the Christian.

"So ought men to love their wives as their own body." (Ephesians 5:23)

"What thing soever I command you, observe to do it: thou shalt not add thereto, nor diminish from it." "Every word of God is pure: he is a shield unto them that put their trust in him. Add thou not unto his words, lest he reprove thee, and thou be found a liar." (Deuteronomy 12:32, Proverbs 30:5-6)

"For I testify unto every man that heareth the words of the prophecy of this book, if any man shall add unto these things, God shall add unto him the plagues that are written in this book:

and if any man shall take away from the words of the book of this prophecy, God shall take away his part out of the book of life, and out of the holy city, and from the things which are written in this book." (Revelation 22:18-19)

These reminders are used often in teaching doctrinal issues of obedience to first principals in becoming a Christian and in rules of worship. The same warnings are appropriate in application to husbands in how they are to respect their wives.

Christ Jesus is first in the life of every Christian. (Matthew 10-:37) There is position, guidance, and assurance for every station within the Faith of Jesus. No one is excluded. The wife is no exception because she is a wife. She is due the respect and consideration due any other believer. Anyone that may have doubts about the issue at hand must answer one question:

Where is the Scripture that teaches it is the husband's duty to force and keep his wife in submission?

CHAPTER SIX

SIX REASONS FOR DEPARTING

Fornication

Covetousness

Idolatry

Railing

Drunkenness

Extortion

CHAPTER SIX

SIX REASONS FOR DEPARTING

"And I say unto you, whosoever shall put away his wife, except it be for fornication, and shall marry another, committeth adultery: and whoso marrieth her which is put away doth commit adultery." (Matthew 19:9)

The majority of believers of the Lord Jesus see Matthew 19:9 as the source Scripture which allows remarriage in the event of divorce by reason of infidelity in the marriage partner.

The instruction given by Jesus and other recorded sayings of Jesus are contained in the part of the Bible known as the New Testament. For that reason most people feel this to be valid instruction under the law of Christ Jesus. This idea is held in religious groups ranging from the most conservative to the most liberal of Christian beliefs.

Again, let it be said, no single verse or phrase of Scripture ever stands alone. Every Bible teaching is well connected and supported by other references. Finding the basis for the question in Matthew 19:3 is necessary to correctly apply the answer.

With the Pharisees being the source and reason for the question, it must be examined from this perspective. They considered themselves **the** authority in godly conduct. In any public appearance they were an ever present element throughout the ministry of Jesus.

Matthew 4:23-25 tells of the power of Jesus and the fame which resulted from the teaching and the healings performed by Him. Because of Jesus' fame, there is no doubt that the Pharisees were aware of the Lord and His doctrine. Their questions were not from a need to know. They feared Jesus because he taught with a knowledgeable and unprecedented authority. (Matthew 7:29)

Early in the recorded teachings of Jesus the problems of divorce and remarriage were discussed. His doctrine was simple and one with which the Pharisees did not agree. The matter of greatest concern for the Pharisees was their desire and effort to find fault with Jesus relative to the Law of Moses and even their own tradition.

Jesus first addressed divorce in the Sermon on the Mount, as recorded in Mathew, Chapter 5. At that time Jesus' fame was spread abroad. This eliminates any doubt about the awareness of the Pharisees when they came to Jesus, tempting Him as recorded in Matthew 19:3 & 7. Included in the arranged plan to tempt the Lord in relation to the Law of Moses, was the effort to excuse their own lack of obedience to the law.

Their disobedience is demonstrated in the question posed on this occasion. "The Pharisees also came unto him, tempting him, and saying unto him, Is it lawful for a man to put away his wife for every cause?" The central question was, "If a man becomes tired of his wife, can he put her away for **any** cause, as judged by the **man** to be sufficient reason?"

Jesus informed them directly from the law, of which they were well aware, when he said, "And I say unto you, "Whosoever shall put away his wife, except it be for fornication, and shall marry another, committeth adultery: and whoso marrieth her which is put away doth commit adultery." (Matthew 19:9)

The questions from the Pharisees were the result of planned entrapment against Jesus. They did not ask questions without first planning their strategy. (Matthew 21:23, 22:15, 34-35, etc.) They knew the Law, the same law they professed to trust and practice. Their problem was one of under estimating the wisdom of Jesus. Added to these things was their desire to avoid the force of the law.

Jesus simply reminded them that Moses allowed divorce for one reason, that being the hardness of their hearts. From the beginning, divorce was not a part of God's plan for mankind.

The Jewish nation practiced not only this, but other activities which were not according to God's preferred wishes for men. Included in those practices was the taking of multiple wives. (Note Matthew 19:4, 5, and 6) God's command was, "Thou shalt not commit adultery" and "thou shalt not covet thy neighbor's wife". (Exodus 20:14-17)

The human mind seems to never cease in its effort to circumvent the benefits of God's wisdom. But the warning is sounded:
"And the times of this ignorance God winked at; but now commandeth all men everywhere to repent. (Acts 17:30)

"And when he was come into his own country, he taught them in their synagogue, in so much that they were astonished, and said, "Whence hath this man this wisdom, and these mighty works? Is not this the carpenter's son? Is not his mother called Mary and his brethren, James, and Joses, and Simon, and Judas? And his sisters, are they not all with us? When then hath this man all these things?" (Matthew 13:55, Mark 6:2)

"And the Jews marveled, saying, How knoweth this man letters, having never learned?" (John 7:15)

The Pharisees, along with other classes of unbelievers, had no respect for the person of Jesus or His educational status. They proved this with their endless questions and suppositions. At the same time they proved themselves false at heart.

The Christian, who would find his Scriptural base in Matthew 19 for remarriage, uses a type of reasoning which allows the innocent party to do in the light what the guilty party did in the dark. That is, seeking companionship outside the original marriage relationship. Jesus said, "From the beginning it was not so".

The passage found in Matthew 19:9 is an answer from the Old Law to people asking questions relating to the Old Law. They had no concept of the New Law and were unable to recognize any authority other than the Law of Moses. They did not believe Jesus even for the miracles he performed. There was even less respect for the message regarding the coming kingdom of heaven. The questions about the Law of Moses require answers from the Law of Moses.

The Law of Moses cannot answer questions directed to the Law of Christ. This distinction surfaces when viewing Matthew 19:9 as the reference for divorce and remarriage. The Law of Moses and the New Testament Law support each other, but, they do not intermingle or overlap. Galatians and Hebrews give invaluable insights about the New Law and its relation to the Old Law.

The New Testament law gives adequate instruction in the matters of marriage and the accompanying problems. Paul writes,
"I say therefore to the unmarried and widows, it is good for them if they abide even as I...But and if thou marry, thou hast not sinned: and if a virgin marry, she hath not sinned. Nevertheless, such shall have trouble in the flesh." (I Corinthians 7)

Those that will marry will have trouble they would not have otherwise. Every situation carries with it, its own particular set of circumstances. Marriage is an ever present part of the human existence as surely as is the circumstances surrounding it. Therefore, marriage and the accompanying problems are given serious consideration in the New Testament Law.

Problems begin with our lack of faith in our Maker to help us choose a mate. How many of us even think to consult the infinite wisdom of God and His Word? Our choices are more often governed by an array of emotional demands such as lust, loneliness, and greed to name a few. Guidance in the Word of the God gives us ground rules before, during, and after marriage. Study and adherence to the Word of God provides complete and perfect answers not only in the choosing, but in issues of divorce and remarriage.

The next subject involves the admonition in I John 2:15-16.
"Love not the world neither the things that are in the world. If any man love the world the love of the Father is not in him. For all that is in the world, the lust of the flesh, and the lust of the eyes, and the pride of life, is not of the Father, but is of the world."

Frequently all of these elements are involved in the process of choosing a lifetime partner. When based on these factors, the thrill of the new relationship falters, and so does the marriage.

The Apostle makes a fair statement about choosing a marriage partner in I Thessalonians 2:3-7. "For this is the will of God, your sanctification: that you abstain from immorality (fornication, K.J.V.); *that each of you know how to take a wife for himself, in holiness and honor, not in the passion of lust* like the heathen who do not know God; (R.S.V.) When the sight is enticed and causes the heart to race, we would do well to seriously consider the long term effects.

Another concern is the purely human tendency to establish differences between male and female in matters of right and wrong, i.e. any particular act is wrong for one gender and not wrong, or sinful, for the other. The Scriptures give witness to this tendency.

A case in point is the woman taken in adultery as recorded in John, chapter 8. In view of the fact that she was taken in the "very act", the Pharisees should have had at least one more person taken in the same "very act." Other than entrapment, their over-riding concern was one of "whom" rather than "what". People allow wrong for one gender and not for the other.

This idea isn't found only in the worldly minded, but also among Christians. It also exists between marriage partners. On too many occasions, fundamental human standards and feelings are found to move into the Church. These are basic concepts common to the natural mind and so strongly ingrained they become accepted as approved by God. The problem is not new. Basic human nature has been used as a correct guide since Adam's first defense of his own sin. Using our own best interest as a guide is as popular now as it was then.

But God sees past our self indulgence. What constitutes sin for one constitutes sin in another. In the eyes of God every soul is of equal value. The same Lord that ransomed one also ransomed the other. It does not matter whether that soul is housed in the male or female temple.

"What: know ye not that your body is the temple of the Holy Spirit which is in you, which ye have of God, and ye are not your own?" (I Corinthians 6:19)

"Know ye not that ye are the temple of God, and the Spirit of God dwelleth in you?" (I Corinthians 3:16)

"For as many of you as have been baptized into Christ have put on Christ. There is neither male nor female; for ye are all one in Christ Jesus." (Galatians 3:27) No gender bias is found here.

Because of these principles, within the body of Christ, the church, we are Christians first. Because of the same standard, we are husband and wife second. Therefore, every instruction of righteousness toward our fellowman, our neighbor, is instruction that readily applies to the marriage partner. There is no reason or excuse for gender prejudice.

The New Testament contains several passages that discuss the marital status. The book of I Corinthians is rich in instruction about the positions of the married and the unmarried, the male and female, of marriage and separation, and the related circumstances.

One passage is held as a key passage in connection to the questions surrounding divorce and remarriage. The passage reads,
"And unto the married I command, yet not I, but the Lord, let not the wife depart from her husband; but if she depart, let her remain unmarried, or be reconciled to her husband; and let not

the husband put away his wife." (I Corinthians 7:10)

In the common church situation, this passage of Scripture is usually read with the reference to the wife placed prominently in view. From such a vantage point, the superficial reading sounds as if the wife decided to leave on a whim, with no thought for Christian responsibility.

Another look at I Corinthians 7:10 reveals a serious, kindly, and generous Christian wife. She loves and cares for her family and husband with conscientious consideration for God's way. She bears long and makes every effort, and then must "depart".

As with any passage of scripture that gives a strong message about right or wrong, good or evil, both parts of I Corinthians 7:10 applies to either gender.

There are numerous guidelines throughout the whole of God's word that are necessary and profitable to the marriage relation. But these teachings are passed over as irrelevant to marriage because direct reference is not made to marriage. They, rather, make direct reference to other relations such as neighbor, brother, friend and foe, or master and servant, etcetera.

In the matter of family breakdown, one very important passage is never given consideration in relation to family living. The passage reads:

"But I have written unto you not to keep company, if any man that is **called** a brother *be* a fornicator, or covetous, or an idolater, or a railer, or a drunkard, or an extortioner; with such an one, no, not to eat." (I Corinthians 5:11)

Keeping in mind that we first belong to Christ, then to husband or wife second, these are the reasons the wife would depart, or the husband would put away his wife. The marriage relationship does not over-ride the relation to the Lord. The family member is due the consideration which is due any other Christian within the church of Christ.

If other members of the body of Christ are not to continue in spiritual fellowship or social contact with such, be they male or female, why should a member of the family, whether spouse or child, be expected to do any more or less? All the offenses named in I Corinthians 5:11 are major in nature. All have a corrosive and deadly effect when dealt with on a regular basis. In a family situation, these things would surely be a source of much greater influence and hardship because of the twenty four hour, close proximity of the offender and the offense.

To the minds of most Bible believing people, I Corinthians 5:11 does not relate to or connect with marriage. It is as if they feel God has provided a Department of Marriage, or a compartment of life separate and apart from the Christian part of one's life.

It is as though certain things apply out of the family which does not apply within the family. This is to say, in essence, the kindness and respect which applies to our neighbor does not apply to our mate. As a result, the instant the marriage contract is completed, there is also instant forfeiting of Christian liberties. This is surely true when both are church members.

It is as if the marriage contract voids all the rules of conduct found in God's Word, except the ones which speak directly to marriage. In the marriage relation, current and customary reasoning turns a blind eye to the extent of differences to be found between human standards and standards found in the faith and doctrine of Jesus.

Marriage is an important matter that requires instruction as surely as any other situation in life. The instruction surrounding marriage is in addition to, not separated from, the remainder of the law of Christ. It goes without saying that every position in life has privileges and limitations. These privileges and limitations require guidance that is clearly outlined in God's Word. The same Word deals with every kind of situation imaginable in the human existence. Marriage does not in any way separate anyone from any part of the benefit of Christ.

Sin of any nature outside of marriage is a sin within marriage. Sin against a neighbor is a sin against a mate. God is no respecter of persons, or of their sins. I Corinthians 5:11 is a clear example of problems found in too many marriages.

Because of long held ideas, traditions, and natural instincts, people often refuse to take the time or any sincere, involved effort to get to the painful nerve center of the things found in I Corinthians 5:11. The study of these particular sins is never done in relation to the marriage situation.

There is an unspoken, but prevailing notion which says if Christians are faithful to God, they most likely won't be subjected to the traumas that happen to the lost. If Christians are subjected to the traumas of the lost, then the Christian must not really be a Christian. Most religious people seem convinced that living the life of faith frees one from the woes of humanity.

As a sad result, we never realize the impact and misery when families are affected directly by the things listed in I Corinthians 5:11. When these things happen to Christians, there is amazement, confusion and embarrassment as to why or how this happened to them. Added to this, through lack of study on these issues, no one is able to offer any truly useful comfort and guidance.

In most religious situations, finger pointing and placing of blame takes over as it did in the case of Job's friends. Frequently the blame is placed on the one that poses the least threat, which is the victim.

There is much unhappiness because the time has not been taken to build a solid foundation from the written word and know the answers before events and emotions become involved and irreversible. Issues and answers continue to be avoided until the situation and people die, either spiritually, physically, or both. To realize the feel of these things, a point by point examination of the effects is worthwhile. I Corinthians 5:11 is a good place to begin connecting the answers.

"But now I have written unto you not to keep company, if any man that is *called* a brother *be* a fornicator, or covetous, or an idolater or a railer, or a drunkard, or an extortioner; with such a one, no, not to eat."

Note the term "called" in this passage. One can be thought to be faithful without being faithful.

The text gives a total of six compelling reasons for parting company with any unfaithful Christian, be they family member or fellow Christian among brethren. In this passage no exceptions are given for family members, whether mate, parents or children.

In the study of the text, it is important to notice the exact wording of the phrase; "…if any man that is **called** a brother be a fornicator, or etcetera, there are definite points of reference involved here. People are very adept at appearing to be one thing when, in fact, they are quite another. Thus the wording, "If any man that is **called** a brother be a fornicator, etcetera". The passage is speaking of someone that is established as "faithful" but living in overt sin, thus leveling a strong influence on the family.

Sin stains not only the guilty individual but those most closely involved. That is the reason there must be a separation from the guilty, regardless of who the Christian is or is not among other Christians.

Fornication must be one of the most prevalent sins of our time. It steals the very life from any marriage and family situation. One guilty of infidelity is willing to expend time, physical energy, moral and spiritual motivation, and financial resources toward this end. Those to whom all these things are rightfully due are surely deprived. Infidelity is one of the greatest causes of marital breakdown. The breakdown then sets the remaining family members adrift in life. Every day we can see examples of the hardship and chaos brought on by the fornicator.

Everything we do in life has stages and growth. To be alert to the temptation of unfaithfulness in the marriage partner, or our own selves, along with the awareness of the Scripture in handling the matter, would save many families from sure destruction. Often there will be a feeling that something isn't right. But we fear finding something amiss and avoid the issue using the excuse of not wanting to judge without sure evidence.

Even if we become aware of the real possibility of unfaithfulness in our mate, most of the time there is an attitude of "wait and see" or "wait to be sure". We seem to be unable or unwilling to move for fear of misjudging. When it is too late to face and possibly correct the problem, self-righteous anger takes full control.

Above and beyond the physical act involved, is the spiritual and emotional significance. The sense of betrayal and desertion is overwhelming. The problems caused by the fornicator are immeasurable in their destruction.

In most any discussion of infidelity, questions usually arise about the differences in adultery and fornication. Sins of immorality will include adultery and fornication. (Galatians 5:19) The Scripture defines each in a such a way that the casual reader will hardly notice. (Note- Romans 7:3, I Corinthians 7:2)

It is interesting to note that adultery isn't listed in I Corinthians 5:11, although it is listed as a definite sin that must be avoided. (I Corinthians

6:9-10) The situation in I Corinthians 5:11, is speaking to things amiss that some may seek to bring in among the people of God after the initial acceptance of the faith. The initial entrance into the faith requires repentance of past sins thus eliminating the adulterer from the church altogether.

Adultery is easily understood from Romans 7:3, while fornication is defined in I Corinthians 5, 6:15-20, 7:2. Loose and aimless sexual activity, including any perverted and indecent use of bodily functions, is an accurate description of fornication as shown by Jude 7. In any event, I Corinthians 5:11 shows the justness and righteousness in seeking separation from the influence of a sinful family member.

Number two on the list is the covetous. "He that is greedy of gain troubleth his own house; but he that hateth gifts shall live". (Proverbs 15:27) The person that is covetous in his heart may covet many different things. Covetousness will usually be discussed in light conversation and the effort to acquire will follow. Another's wife or husband is often among those things coveted.

Are we to suppose this is a matter to be taken lightly? Many jokes are made about such things with no discussion in the way of encouragement toward correct conduct.

"Fools make a mock at sin;" (Proverbs 14:9)

The burning desire for that which one does not possess is the cause of many additional kinds of crimes. Covetousness, the desire for things not owned, can also be defined as greed over that which is already in possession. (Luke 12:15, I Samuel 25:1-11)

Everyone has needs and wants. To live daily in an intimate situation with one that is heavily supplied, while others are in desperate need leaves just cause for deep and bitter resentment. This deficiency in an individual causes members of the family to suffer many hardships of physical, psychological and spiritual deprivation. The damages caused are difficult to identify and measure by those outside an intimate relationship. Part of the difficulty in identifying the problem comes from fear of finding oneself in the position of being accused of meddling in family affairs and attacked personally.

Imagine the father who keeps himself well supplied in cars and hobbies while the family goes lacking in food and clothing: The mother who freely spends time and money on herself, depriving her family of care and attention. Any member of the family, whether male or female, with the problem of over indulgence is a burden to all concerned.

Covetousness causes the sin of indulgence to the destruction of others. Some of the deadliest effects are born by the family. None should suppose this is a matter to be taken lightly by the church simply because it does not affect them directly.
"But godliness with contentment is great gain. For we brought nothing into this world, and it is certain we can carry nothing out. And having food and raiment, let us be therefore content, but they that will be rich fall into temptation and a snare, and into many foolish and hurtful lusts, which drown men in destruction and perdition. For the love of money is the root of all evil: which while some coveted after, they have erred from the faith, and pierced themselves through with many sorrows." (I Timothy 6:6-10)
One's family is also pierced through by the covetous person.

Covetousness is a large and pervasive sin among the religious leaders of the present time. It is manifested in the material wealth and exhibited through grand and marvelous religious structures and high living of leaders. The New Testament epistles give frequent warnings about covetousness. There is no lack of Scripture on the subject. But religious leaders use the scriptures to encourage the giving of funds, "that they with feigned words shall make merchandise of you". (II Peter 2:1-3)

Covetousness is shown in many forms and is persistent in the human species. The proof of this is evident in the lack of teaching on the subject. It is also synonymous with idolatry. (Colossians 3:5)

"Mortify therefore your members which are upon the earth; fornication, uncleanness, inordinate affection, evil concupiscence, and covetousness, which is idolatry."

Number three on the list of offenders is the idolater. Today's idolater has as many idols as any of the ancient peoples. (Acts 17:16) The greater difference being the material or physical form.

Desire for power and fame are also matters of idolatry. Placing oneself in the position of the idol doesn't lessen this particular sin. The idol of material gain, or worldly approval, or any all consuming passion, is as much a detriment to a family situation, as to the church. This type of individual can include one who spends every waking hour engaged in gainful employment. He has no time for God, family, or neighbors.

The idolater, in their most rank sense, would not be one which any faithful Christian would be required to share daily living. This has caused the most wise and mighty of men to commit great sins against the God whom they professed to love and trust. What passage of Scripture can be found commanding one to cling to such a person simply because they are in the position of being a family member?

Any idolater who would fall down to worship an image would be an unrighteous influence within a family unit as well as within the church as a whole. The family unit is a part of the church. Paul writes,
"Wherefore, my dearly beloved, flee from idolatry." (I Corinthians 10:14) John wrote,
"Little children, keep yourselves from idols." I John 5:21)
Neither John nor Paul make any exceptions for family members.

Not only does this affect the immediate family, but also the church. The effects placed upon the family will give direct flow into the church. This flow is sure because of the misery and conflict brought on the family members remaining in fellowship.

In addition, it is much easier for the transgressor to continue in transgression when the family unit remains as a safe harbor. As long as there is a connection to the familiar there is little incentive to repent. This allows the transgressor to enjoy both situations.

In allowing the offending individual the luxury of all the comforts of home, the hardening of the heart progresses at a slower, more permanent pace. Drifting from a position of the familiar into danger lets the transgressor grow accustomed and comfortable without the shock of instant reality and loss.

Number four on the list is the railer. This transgression is described in several appropriate terms. These include such terms as backbiting, reviling, scoffing, mocking, false accusations, and maliciousness, to name a few. Railing involves the tone of voice and facial expression in its execution. Although the primary source of this activity is the mouth, the complete physical demeanor is involved in various ways.

Railing is an act committed, either in jest, in a humorous form or with anger. To scoff or mock will carry the idea of light, sarcastic remarks designed to bring about unfounded prejudices. The act causes the inventing of exaggerated words and actions intended to excite contemptuous laughter. These are a great part of the sin of railing.

"And they that passed by railed on him, wagging their heads, and saying, Ah, thou that destroyest the temple, and buildest it in three days, save thyself, and come down from the cross". (Mark 15:29-32)

This instance of the sin of railing is one of the most sad and foolish. Little men mocking the intrinsic gift of an all powerful and loving Father is profound cause for fear.

When railing is carried out with anger, the result is harshness and thoughtlessness. Any act within this realm includes false accusations and exaggerated fault finding. Many times the victim is made to feel guilt for things over which there is no personal control and often no awareness.

The railer will place blame on another for that which is lacking in their own character. One frequent example says, "If you had not done this, I would not have been forced to do that." The railer is alert to ways of placing the blame for their mistakes at the door of whoever is convenient.

It is a notorious weapon of intimidation and humiliation. It is willful and often pointless mental and emotional pain that is to no purpose and never allowed to heal. Railing is a secret and subtle tool of control within a family. It is frequently the casting of one's personal feelings of guilt on to another in grievous and harsh terms.

The sin of railing is that in which one person feels self gratification and justification in the deed. The railer blames his actions on the perceived faults and weaknesses of others.

The railer, being aware of his guilt, avoids responsibility and accountability by transferring his guilt onto someone whom he knows will meekly accept that responsibility. Railing, shrouded in guilt, shame, need, and a multitude of other character flaws, is one of the most elusive and undetectable sins. It is a subtle but harsh act. This is especially true within the family. The railer is one who does not forgive.

This is one sin that has not been discussed to any length in Bible study classes. Yet it is often used in the privacy of the home. The victim is left with confusion and doubt in how to make things right. Its effect is most detrimental within the family unit.

The drunkard is number five in order. The drunkard needs no introduction. Most everyone knows one somewhere in their own or some other family. Testimony is readily available as to the havoc left in the wake of a drunkard. The person's inner-self as well as involvement in employment, family, church, or social activities are left in shambles.

For the sake of clarification, it is necessary to be aware that drunkenness can be as subtle as any other weakness. When thinking in general terms of a drunkard, it is with the image of one that staggers and is disoriented. This individual's destruction of himself and those whose lives he touches is obvious. The social or casual drinker, who appears to remain "in control", is just as destructive, albeit a slower, longer process. Social drinkers do not appear to be drunk, least of all to themselves. However, their path leads to the same indisputable destination.

The casual and not quite addicted drinker should take thought of those that require ten drinks to become drunk. The first drink leaves them about one tenth drunk. They are on their way as surely as the obvious staggering drunk.

A drunkard is necessarily measured by the amount and the product consumed. From that point, it is simply a matter of the rate of progress to reach the same final destination.

Much is said of illness in connection with drunkenness. Addiction to anything that destroys body and soul is surely an illness for anyone, including those related to the person so entrapped.
"At the last it biteth like a serpent, stingeth like an adder." (Proverbs 23:32)
This is the warning from God of the dangers of alcohol.

Number six on the list is the extortioner. Extortion is the use of legal or illegal authority for excess legal or illegal gain or control. Extortion involves deception, threatening and overt force. Extortion is more often seen as a crime of large proportions among the criminal elements, or being carried out in business in the form of exorbitant charges for services and goods. Religious situations are rampant with extortion under the guise of collections and solicitation for monies.

Extortion is also found within the home and family. The home is not a democracy. There are the weaker, the stronger, the dependant and the independent. Numerous crimes are committed in the privacy of the home.

The idea of extortion as a dimension in family life is one that appears in many forms, especially as it applies to a man over a woman or children. In the normally accepted thought line, in religious and church situations, the women are the yielding element, the women being thought of as the "weaker" gender.

It is interesting that in any major religion, Christian or not, one cornerstone of their doctrine is the subservience of their women to the men. This is another form of extortion. One person extorts another's daily life simply by expecting them to meet their demands.

According to I Corinthians 5:11, the fornicator, the covetous, the idolater, the railer, the drunkard, the extortioner, is cause for the wife to depart or the husband to put away his wife. God's word makes no distinction as to whom the Christian may be related. Paul said simply,

"...therefore put away from among yourselves that wicked person." (I Corinthians 5:13)

In returning to the problem of marital separation, some people believe that once married, separation or divorce under any circumstance is a sin. However, I Corinthians 5:11 clearly states the terms dictating the departing of the wife or the husband putting away his wife. What most people don't understand is I Corinthians 5:11 applies to family members as well as church members. The customary consensus is that these terms apply only to the general church population.

The Christian who will return to the old life of sin will often do so with an over-powering show of will. With the masculine gender, the natural instinct doesn't normally allow him to relinquish control over those things he considers as belonging to him, including a wife and family.

Then the problem of remarriage enters the picture. I Corinthians 7:11 states specifically there is to be no remarriage to another. Romans 7:3-4 will also show this to be the commandment. But in these times of moral laxness, situations and circumstances arise that no segment of humanity seems able to resist.

In too many instances, the second marriage is looked upon as imperative. The mind is focused upon the idea that the human existence requires companionship. In today's society, as well as in most religious positions, intimacy is politely accepted as necessary. But every matter in our personal life is ours to control properly even though we may think it can't be done. (I Corinthians 10:13)

"Have ye not read, that he which made them at the beginning made them male and female, and said, for this cause shall a man leave his father and mother, and shall cleave to his wife; and they twain shall be one flesh?" (Matthew 19:5-6)

Most readers will take notice of the phrase, "They twain shall be one flesh" as being a rather loosely bound idea, having to do mostly with the physically intimate act. Because of this type of thinking many forget the weightier matters of mutual friendship, common interests, and common spiritual beliefs.

"so ought men to love their wives as their own bodies. He that loveth his wife loveth himself. For no man ever yet hated his own flesh; but nourisheth and cherisheth it even as the Lord the church." (Ephesians 5:28)

This doesn't sound so loosely stated. In remarriage it is rather the beginning of another chapter with the same characters, the same problems, with additional characters and problems. The truth of this is stronger than ever when children are involved.

Divorce and a second marriage do not end the first marriage. It doesn't matter how long we live, or where we go, the marital status colors every other situation in life. The effects of separation and divorce will travel through the span of a lifetime and beyond. In contemplating marriage and/or remarriage, people suffer self-deception, self-defeat, and ultimately, self-destruction.

It is difficult to accept and adjust after a family break-up. Many people are involved in many types of martial conflicts resulting in permanent damage to body and mind. Divorce is not the least of these.

A loss of limb or some other part of the physical body compares closely to the marriage relationship. None would dare to cut off the damaged part of the body, throw it away, and then rush out to begin looking for that which belongs to another to claim for his own. (Remember, "...and they shall become one flesh.) Through God's word, the marriage relation is shown to be as close and connected as the body with each of its parts.

"For this cause shall a man leave his father and mother, and shall be joined unto his wife, and they two shall be one flesh." (Ephesians 5:31)

We have many hopes and plans in this life for completeness, but Satan is among us to try our faith at every turn. Subverting God's word was the first device. (Genesis 3:4) This device continues to work very well in the marriage scenario. All it takes is one well placed error to go unnoticed. In this instance, it is the misplacing and misuse of one verse of Scripture, namely, Matthew 19:9. The misapplication of this one passage lets people feel there is a crack to squeeze through should the desire arise. Much suffering comes from problems entering the marriage situation. But suffering doesn't nullify God's laws.

The New Testament law, the law of Christ tells of one allowance for remarriage. The one reason is the death of the marriage partner. Even then, there is a close restriction in that another partner is to be a fellow Christian.

"The wife is bound by the law as long as her husband liveth; but if her husband be dead, she is at liberty to be married to whom she will; **only in the Lord.**" (I Corinthians 7:39)

It goes without saying, in the same situations, that which applies to the woman also applies to the man. Every commandment of righteousness in the Lord always applies equally to every soul. God is no respecter of gender. To abide by these simple, to-the-point, rules, is to be faithful to God's laws and the simplicity which is in Christ.

Without fail, I Corinthians 7:15 is used to full advantage in saying,
"But if the unbelieving depart, let him depart. A brother or sister is not under bondage in such cases: but God hath called us to peace."
Within most church congregations, this passage is used to show justification in allowing remarriage for anyone that has been wronged in marriage. Indeed, the offender is often treated as an alien sinner, regardless of former standing as a Christian. This is a tactic to allow the offended Christian the freedom to remarry. Scripture doesn't sanction this type of maneuvering by any stretch of the imagination.

People assume the phrase "not under bondage" allows them a great deal of freedom. The feeling is that once a person is free from any sort of daily duties involved in a pre-existing marriage, the person is then free to do whatever he chooses in becoming involved in another state of "bondage" or responsibility within another marriage.

But the usage of I Corinthians 7:15 must remain within the context for correct understanding and application. Within the context, I Corinthians 7:15 deals specifically with the obligations of the believer that is converted within the marriage, while the other maintains the position of unbeliever. Therefore, if and when the unbelieving partner departs, that is the choice of that individual. God's word is simply saying the Christian part of the marriage cannot be held responsible for the decision of the unbelieving part.

Once the unbeliever departs, this does not leave the door open for the believer to become responsible, or "in bondage" in another marriage. Romans 7:3 and I Corinthians 7:39 are as strong as ever. It is as binding for the believer as the unbeliever. Maintaining the status of "unbeliever" does not make one unaccountable. "All shall stand before God and give account for the deeds done in the flesh." (Romans 2:6, 14:10, Revelation 20:22)

Because one is not a believer makes him no less accountable to God's word. The great difference between the believer and the unbeliever is the believer is accountable before the church.(I Corinthians 5:12-13,6:1-6) Both are accountable to God in the final analysis. Paul is saying the believer is not held accountable for the actions of the departing unbeliever. It is simply a matter of realizing that God is not unreasonable. He does not hold one in bondage, or responsible, or accountable for the deeds of another, be they believer or unbeliever.

Often the teachings of Jesus seem harsh not only to unbelievers but also to believers. (John 6:60) Likewise, the instructions found in the letters of the Apostles are direct and to the point with regard to marriage, divorce and remarriage.

In ignorance of God's guidance in the marriage situation, people will frequently divorce and remarry. When truth comes to their attention, then they want and expect forgiveness while maintaining the second marriage. The encouragements of God in His commandments does not leave any doubt about what constitutes righteous and unrighteous deeds, whether in or out of marriage.

Praying for forgiveness, while maintaining a wrong situation of any nature after we find the truth, is asking God to make an exception in our case. God the Father has made no promise and offers no hope in this. Acting in ignorance is not offered any exceptions. The command is to repent and turn from ignorance and the sin that is the result of ignorance.

"And the times of this ignorance God winked at; but now commandeth all men every where to repent:" (Acts 17:30)

Provisions were given in the Law of Moses for sin committed in ignorance. (Leviticus 4:2, Numbers 5: 24-30) Within the law of Jesus Christ, ignorance is recognized and the command is to repent. Then for Christians, repentance and prayer is the remedy. (Acts 8:22) In dealing with different problems, the Apostle Paul writes,

"But I would not have you ignorant, brethren….." (I Corinthians 10:1, I Thessalonians 4:13) "Study to show thyself approved", "Give thyself to reading", "prove all things, and hold fast to that which is good". The encouragement and instruction is abundant. Ignorance and error are closely related. Neither is an equitable excuse for continuing on a wrong path.

Those that are "unlearned and unstable" remain so "to their own destruction". (II Peter 3:16) The teaching and encouragement is to "Study to show thyself approved unto God", whether it is marriage, divorce, or any other matter relating to marriage or divorce. (II Timothy 2:15)

Repentance is not easy when it is related to marriage. This is due in part to the pervasive weaknesses in human nature. Yet, the same people who cannot see a way to separate themselves from an immoral relationship for the sake of their eternal soul, will separate for almost any other reason of much less value. The revealed will of God gives freedom from the first marriage to marry a second time, only by reason of death.

The Lord Jesus was aware of human nature when he said, "And if thy right eye offend thee…". Matthew 5:27-30 tells of the difficulty of this problem and the difficulty of repenting of a wrong position in marriage. When there are children involved, the situation is all the more complicated. It is difficult for people to accept that repenting of a sinful marriage requires ending that marriage.

People want to think that surely the Lord would not require such a thing when people are deeply in love and even have children. However, these passages must be considered: Matthew 5:28-29, 10:37, I Corinthians 10:6. Ezra, chapter three, reveals an actual account of just such an event.

There is no doubt the general marriage situation is in a shambles with all the attendant misery. God is not the perpetrator of this misery. How many of us honestly thought to ask His help in choosing a lifetime mate? How many will humble themselves to ask God's help in surviving the trials that arise? The answers are self evident.

Usually, the first step in seeking a marriage partner is to 'fall in love'. In the search, we allow our emotions to be our guide. In no other situation in life do we so willingly "fall" into anything which has such long term consequences as the marriage agreement. To 'fall in love' has the ring of falling into a pit. Many times, that is exactly the end result.

In nothing else so serious, so important, so close to the heart and soul, do we behave with such abandon. The abandonment is practiced in our choice of one that has so much power over our happiness, or conversely over our misery. If misery is the result, it is then and only then we want to cry out to God. Then we, as Christians, want God's help to let us out of the contract we ourselves have so tightly fashioned.

God is a loving Father and His complete will is always available. This is taken so much for granted. "...because that which may be known of God is manifest in them; for God hath showed it unto them...so that they are without excuse:" (Romans 1:18-20) Because most people take the availability of the will of God for granted, there is much neglect in seeking those careful guidelines. When life becomes unbearable or when God's will is understood, then the usual tactic is to search out the phrase of Scripture that appears to allow for maneuvering into the desired position.

In marrying and giving in marriage, there is a duty we owe ourselves. This duty is to be aware of placing ourselves in the position of, "The foolish man (that) perverteth his way and in his heart fretteth against the Lord." (Proverb 19:3) So often people will ask, "Why does God let these things happen?", when they have personally brought it about by failing to abide by God's instructions.

When God's instructions regarding divorce and remarriage are taught versus commonly held practices, people become defensive, argumentative and rail against being judged. God's truth on the matter has not changed. Many are those who are directly affected by divorce. This makes the subject extremely hard to deal with in an objective manner.

This life is given to us as a time for making decisions. Most decisions are made without the knowledge of God's will. Therefore we are found in the position of not realizing the immediate and the eternal ramifications of the action.

"At the times of this ignorance God winked at; but now commandeth all men every where to repent: because he hath appointed a day, in the which he will judge the world in righteousness by that man whom he hath ordained whereof he hath given assurance unto all men, in that he hath raised him from the dead." Acts 17:30-33) Through the resurrection of Jesus, God has assured everyone that His word is true in every respect.

"For the wrath of God is revealed from heaven against all ungodliness and unrighteousness of men, who hold the truth in unrighteousness; because that which may be known of God is manifest in them; for God hath showed it unto them." (Romans 1:18-19)

Many and countless are those who find themselves in the situation of remarriage after divorce. It is not an unfamiliar situation, nor unique to our life and time. The time of Noah was rampant with this same problem among the people of God. This was one of the chief causes for the flood being brought on the world. (Genesis 6:1-4) Whether in that time or this, the problem of marriage after divorce is a moral issue with moral as well as spiritual consequences that we cannot avoid.

"For if we would judge ourselves, we should not be judged. But when we are judged, we are chastened of the Lord, that we should not be condemned with the world. (I Corinthians 11:31)

Divorce and remarriage touches every one of us in some painful way. Thus, unbiased and objective search of God's word is made extremely difficult. Strong emotions hinder the study and affect the commitment to righteous solutions.

This study is done with strong sympathy and compassion for those who may be so entangled with loved ones thus involved.

Yet the matter does not allow the use of Matthew 19:9 as a way of finding new companionship when we feel the need or desire. Matthew 19:9 is instruction from the Law of Moses to those people who were subject to that Law. Christians in the faith of Christ cannot claim this as a basis for divorce and remarriage for any reason. It is not a part of the Christian system as taught by the Apostles through the guidance of the Holy Spirit.

Chapter Seven

OPINION, OPTION, and EXPEDIENCY

The Religious Arena Has an Excess of Opinion

Opinion Governs Large and Small Matters

Silence in God's Word Not Seriously Considered

CHAPTER SEVEN
OPINION, OPTION AND EXPEDIENCY

Webster's dictionary defines opinion as, "belief stronger than impression and less strong then positive knowledge". Option is defined as, "the power of choice". Expediency is defined as, "that which is fitting for the purpose".

Opinion enters into matters of faith and worship to God where it is thought that options are open. When it is felt that options are open to opinion, the opinion often becomes conviction. The greater the number of people supporting the opinion, the stronger the conviction.

In the event of doubt or inquiry into the questioned opinions, the small things will seem too small to merit serious concern. Other matters of greater dimension are not questioned because of their apparent importance.

The religious or spiritual arena has more than its share of practices based in small and great matters of opinion. Practices formed from opinion are found in every denomination. Opinion is even found among those who have a strong desire to pattern their teachings closely to the doctrine of Christ.

When it is believed that the Scripture doesn't offer a clear command to do or not to do in certain areas, opinions are frequently allowed to become binding law. Many of these beliefs have existed over long periods of time. Because of long term acceptance, such practices appear to be the righteousness of God.

One example of opinion allowed as valid belief, in what appears to be an unimportant thing, involves the preaching of the first gospel sermon. There is a problem of understanding how one man could preach one sermon to so many different language groups at the same time. The topic of the first sermon is frequently discussed, but some of the details of how this was accomplished are more or less allowed to fall by the wayside. Opinion answers the matter of one man, namely the Apostle Peter, being able to preach one sermon to people "out of every nation under heaven" in one single instance. (Acts 2:5)

The proposal is usually made to the effect that a miracle of some description was given for the hearing and comprehension of those listening to Peter. Note is taken of the passage that discusses the astonishment of the multitude. Acts 2:6-11 reads,

"Now when this was noised abroad, the multitude came together and were confounded, because that every man heard them speak in his own language. And they were all amazed and marveled, saying one to another, Behold, are not all these which speak Galileans? and how hear we every man in our own tongue, wherein we were born?.. .we do hear them speak in our tongues the wonderful works of God?"

The puzzle begins to unravel in Acts 2:11. It says, "we do hear them speak in our tongues the wonderful works of God." This tells of eleven of the apostles speaking in all the languages present among the multitude. Also, the subject of discussion is revealed. This subject was "the wonderful works of God". Acts 2:14 then states, "But Peter, standing up with the eleven, lifted up his voice....."

Those things spoken in the several languages by the apostles were not the preaching of the gospel in this particular instance. It was exactly what it says; "All these which speak" were Galileans. (Acts 2:7 They were speaking, "in our tongues the wonderful works of God". The contents of the things said about "the wonderful works of God" are not revealed. The message content that is revealed is the message that everyone heard as "Peter stood up with the eleven".

The thing that everyone heard from the one speaker, with common understanding, was the gospel message. The one message was preached by one man, Peter. He was promised the privilege when Jesus said to him, ". . .and I will give unto thee the keys of the kingdom of heaven:" (Matthew 16:16-19). This promise was made to Peter only, and not to the eleven other apostles. So the question is, how did one man preach to so many different language groups at one time, with everyone understanding so completely?

The answer lies in the fact that all the listeners were Jewish. They were

Jewish by birth, by faith, by practice, and national heritage.

The Jews were a conquered nation. This was the position they had endured over a long period of time. Because they had been captive, and in many instances, dispersed throughout the known world, they were accustomed to, and practiced, in the native languages of the countries in which they were living. This is apparent because of the presence of, "Jews, devout men, out of every nation under heaven". (Acts 2:5)

Other nations of people do not realize what it means to be Jewish. There isn't a realistic awareness of the separation maintained by the Jews between themselves and the remainder of the world's population.

There also isn't any realistic awareness of the mannerisms and customs which constitute or make up the separation. Nor are the majority of people outside the Jewish community aware of the standards involved in preserving the closely guarded separation. One key requirement in safeguarding Jewish ties is that every one be schooled in the Hebrew language. (Acts 22:2)

Who, but devout Jews, would have been in Jerusalem for one of the highest Jewish holy days? The Prophets were quoted extensively in the first gospel message. Only the Hebrew speaking people would be readily familiar with these prophets.

Several other verses in Acts illustrate that Jews made up the listening audience. "ye men of Judea" (Acts 2:14), Ye men of Israel (Acts 2:22), "Men and brethren (Acts 2: 29), Men and brethren (Acts 2:37). The gospel was promised first to the Jews. In every example, the apostles spoke to the Jewish nation before turning to the Gentiles. (Acts 13:46, 18:6)

All those that heard were Jews. All were Hebrew speaking people. The Apostle Peter was a Hebrew. He preached to Hebrew people in the language of the Hebrews. There are no mysteries surrounding the delivery and acceptance of the first gospel sermon. There is no place for conjecture or opinion.

Opinion is the troublesome element that creates error. Surface reading of the Scripture often gives rise to opinions in many areas of Bible teaching. These are easy to come by when some particular passage appears simple and seems to need no serious consideration to gain an understanding. I Corinthians 6:4 is one such passage. "If then ye have judgments of things pertaining to this life, set them to judge who are least esteemed in the church."

In this day of status consciousness, the first thought abhors the idea of "setting those least esteemed" in judgment. Surface reading seems easy enough to understand when left as it appears without comparing similar or explanatory references. With I Corinthians 6:4 left as it appears it isn't even taken too seriously. Because of the lack of use, it is hardly functional.

This passage of Scripture is rarely if ever, quoted in any lesson material or applied to any particular situation. Yet the wording and context shows it to be pointed and straight forward instruction.

The casual reading sounds as though the passage is saying something about some among the brotherhood who are held as less worthy or not too highly regarded. But this wouldn't be correct because Philippians 2:3 and James 2 rejects favoritism and high-mindedness among Christians.

"Dare any of you, having a matter against another, go to law before the unjust, and not before the saints? Do ye not know that the saints shall judge the world? and if the world shall be judged by you, are ye unworthy to judge the smallest matters? Know ye not that we shall judge angels? How much more things that pertain to this life? If then ye have judgments of things pertaining to this life, set them to judge who are least esteemed in the church." (I Corinthians 6:1-4)

The information in this passage is one of the guidelines in governing the church. It is a command. It is straight forward, with few words. It is information that involves disputes about moral behavior, and the judgment of these matters. The particular problem for consideration in this passage is one of a brother within the church cheating other brethren.

"I speak to your shame. Is it so, that there is not a wise man among you? No, not one that shall be able to judge between his brethren? but brother goeth to law with brother, and that before the unbelievers. Now therefore there is utterly a fault among you, because ye go to law one with another. Why do ye not rather take wrong? Why do ye not rather suffer yourselves to be defrauded? nay, ye do wrong and defraud, and that your brethren." (I Corinthians 6:5-8)

The rebuke is fourfold. The first rebuke is for the Christian who would go to law before unbelievers against a fellow Christian. The second rebuke is for the Christian's lack of ability to judge between brethren in their conduct toward one another. The third rebuke is for the lack of ability to suffer injustice. The forth rebuke is for those who will defraud another.

The meaning and usage of I Corinthians 6:4 would necessarily be considered in the light of any matter demanding judgment. "If then ye have judgments of things pertaining to this life, set them to judge who are least esteemed in the church." The phrase that is in question reads, "set them to judge who are least esteemed in the church."

At this point it seems the reasonable understanding means that "those least esteemed in the church" is the same as, or means, "those least associated" with the dispute or question needing "judgment". There is a dispute between brethren that needs unbiased assistance from sources outside the parties immediately involved. And there is the need for each side to present its case without fear of bias or prior judgment.

The same system of judgment can be observed in the courts of America. Within the church and the population in general, disputes and misunderstandings will arise. With disputes and disagreements, there arises the need for a system that will render peaceful and equitable decisions.

I Corinthians 6:4 requires the understanding and use remain in the context in which it is written. The text involves righteousness and judgment within the body, the church of Christ.

Certain single Bible terms are also given shallow attention. Included in this is the common misuse of the passages involving faith. As a result people often demonstrate a faith in their faith to save their souls in eternity. Whether their faith is founded in the Bible doctrine of faith or not, seems to have little connection with the basis of their faith. They believe in their own ability to believe strongly enough in God, to save them. Because of faith in this confidence, they hope to attain salvation.

The term "faith" is a word that moves easily between points of usage. Determining how and which points apply in any particular passage, is worthy of serious consideration.

Several passages containing the word 'faith' are often used only to show the importance of our faith toward God. Comparing other related passages shows the greater depths of these passages. One often used example is found in several places in the Bible. This familiar passage says, "The just shall live by faith".

This quote is used to teach the necessity of faith or trust, on our part, toward God. It seems to fit and it sounds good. But is the passage saying this every time?

One passage found in Habakkuk reads, "But the just shall live by his faith". Other passages that make the similar quote read, "the just shall live by faith". These two quotes sound almost alike. There is one word, (his) that can make a vast difference in the final content of the message found in any particular passage.

There is no doubt that we must have faith (belief) within our hearts. It is also without doubt that our faith must be grounded and settled in the faith (teaching) of the Word.

"Faith cometh by hearing, and hearing by the word of God." (Romans 10:17)

"There is one body, one Spirit, one Lord, one faith..." (Ephesians 4:4—6) "Examine yourselves, whether ye be in the faith; prove your own selves:" (II Corinthians 13:5) '...and let us run with patience the race that is set before us, looking unto Jesus the author and finisher of our faith. . ." (Hebrews 12:2)

"Beloved, when I gave all diligence to write unto you of the common salvation, it was needful for me to write unto you, and exhort you that ye should earnestly contend for the faith which was once delivered unto the saints." (Jude 3)

The "faith of Christ" (Philippians 3:9) is the "doctrine of Christ" (I Timothy 4:6) is the "doctrine of God" (I Timothy 6:1), which is "the Word". (I Timothy 5:17)

The faith of any individual may be little or much in strength. The faith (belief) of any value is grounded and settled in the faith (doctrine) of Christ.

"...for therein is the righteousness of God revealed from faith to faith: as it is written, the just shall live by faith." (Romans 1:17)

Too frequently people do not investigate the fact that without the written Faith, we have no faith. Select areas of belief and practice are subject to the practice of believing the unrevealed. This is because it is thought that the Scripture has not given guidance in some matters that people think are important necessities. Nevertheless it is written,

"The word is nigh thee, even in thy mouth, and in thy heart: that is the word of faith, which we preach; (Romans 10:8)

The Faith "the just shall live by" is the Faith found in the written will of Christ. Faith in any other that is less, more or different from the Faith of Christ is futile.

Many different things are taught, as matters of utmost importance, for doctrines of faith in religion. Evidence of this fact is shown by the different and contradictory practices among the spiritual minded. These are often things, which in reality, are not remotely connected to the revealed Faith found in God's Word.

"He who hath ears to hear, let him hear." (Matthew 13:43) "But in vain they do worship me, teaching for doctrines the commandments of men." (Matthew 15:9)

The faith shown from our hearts must conform to the written, the revealed faith, found in God's word.

"And be not conformed to the world; but be ye transformed by the renewing of your mind, that ye may approve what is that good, and acceptable, and perfect will of God." (Romans 12:2) In every thing our faith must be maintained within the bounds of the written Faith of Jesus.

The area where opinions abound is in the areas known as the silence of God's word. The amount of teaching about this subject is small when compared to the teaching pertaining to other topics such as faith, obedience, hope, or any of the on-going points of doctrine.

God's word calls the unrevealed things "the secret things". "The secret things belong unto the Lord our God: but those things which are revealed belong unto us and to our children forever, that we may do all the words of this law."(Deuteronomy 29:29)

The "silence" or "secret things of God" have existed in every dispensation of time.

In worship to God, there are things thought to be important which are not revealed. These matters are not brought forward by revelation from God's word, but by opinion. These are things that enter through the avenue of logic and preference, or option.

Matters of opinion in faith toward God aren't limited to this day and time. People have been subject to the problem since the beginning of man's existence on earth. One later example is found in the great king David, of the nation of Israel. Although he is called 'a man after God's own heart:" (Acts 13:22), David was not above doing things his way.

One of the notable examples of David resorting to opinion was the decision to build the temple. "And it came to pass, when the king sat in his house, and the Lord had given him rest round about from all his enemies; that the king said unto Nathan the prophet, See now, I dwell in a house of cedar, but the ark of God dwelleth within curtains." (II Samuel 7:13).

David was long accustomed to vigilance as a shepherd and later as an accomplished warrior. His life had involved an abundance of enterprise and energetic action. Now all was peaceful and secure. Routine had set in. So David sat musing and daydreaming. Too much calm and tranquility soon becomes annoying for a man accustomed to constant change.

"Nathan the prophet said to the king, Go, do all that is in thine heart; for the Lord is with thee." Nathan thought it sounded like a good idea. There wasn't any moral sin involved. There wasn't any interference with any commandments of worship of the Law. To the mortal mind, anything that does not involve moral sin, or if it doesn't appear to interfere with the commandments of worship, it is considered permissible. In this instance, it sounded like the reasonable thing to do. But what did the Lord God say to this logical idea?

"Howbeit the Most High dwelleth not in temples made with hands; as saith the prophet, Heaven is my throne, and earth is my footstool; what house will ye build me? saith the Lord: or what is the place of my rest? Hath not my hand made all these things? Ye stiffnecked and uncircumcised in heart and ears, ye do always resist the Holy Ghost: as your fathers did, so do ye." (II Samuel 7:1–7, Acts 7:44–51)

The Lord was not unaware of the coming desire to build the temple. The idea for the effort came under the same heading as the desire for a king. (Deuteronomy 17:14, I Samuel 8) Not only this, but temples of the heathen idols were impressive structures. No doubt Israel would see an essential need for the same standard for the ark of God. (Compare with I Samuel 8:5)

Added to David's desire to build the temple was a sense of guilt. The king now lived in a house of cedar while the ark of God dwelled in a tent. David was a man of humble beginnings. He was capable of an appreciation of the finer material things of life. Upon reaping the benefits of being king over God's people, it was possible for a misplaced sense of guilt to overwhelm him.

The question arises as to why the temple was built and this with explicit instructions from God Himself. The same answer can be given as for other things which did not come from divine commandment.

Some of the other things allowed included divorce, the taking of multiple wives (which amounts to effectively putting away the first wife), the setting up of a king, and the taking of slaves. When asked about one of these issues, Jesus informed the Pharisees "...because of the hardness of your hearts...". (Matthew 19:8)

The Apostle Paul calls any act beyond the revealed Word, an act of ignorance and vanity. (Acts 14:30-31, 16:30)

The temple was an impressive structure, even by today's standards. From the material point of view, it was far superior to the tabernacle constructed at the direction of Moses in the wilderness. But, for all this, God didn't seem impressed with the idea.

The book of Hebrews quietly brings this to the front. This book was written for the purpose of showing the superiority of Christ and the gospel, above the tabernacle and the Law of Moses. In bringing the comparisons to light, the tabernacle is discussed thoroughly. But the temple, in and of its self, is never mentioned in any fashion in the entire book of Hebrews. The tabernacle is shown as the example and shadow of heavenly things, while the temple is not given any degree of recognition.

There is a lesson here for our time. The obvious thing is that the whole idea of the tabernacle originated with God. The idea of the temple originated from man. But God had a purpose for the temple.

Because of the purpose of God, it is written, "Then David gave to Solomon his son the pattern of the porch...and the pattern of all that he had by the Spirit...of service in the house of the Lord. . .All this, said David, the Lord made me understand in writing by his hand upon me, even all the works of this pattern." "For the palace is not for man, but for the Lord God." (I Chronicles 28:29, 29:1)

After the building of the first temple, the Jewish leaders were convinced that the temple was a necessary part of the Jewish system of worship. They were dedicated to reconstruction each time the temple was destroyed. However this was not without the purpose of God.

God's word teaches through three avenues. These three avenues come through direct commandments, examples shown, and principles brought forward as the result of commandments and examples. No doubt there are necessary conclusions to be realized as a result of principles which are taught, but this is an area which is due extreme caution. Instead of caution, the necessary inference frequently becomes the necessary standard. 'Necessary inference' and 'necessary conclusion' are not one in the same.

It is common practice among religious people to add this fourth dimension known as the 'Necessary Inference'. The necessary inference, by definition, is a conclusion reached as the result of logical reasoning.

Through this standard, the ideas of people are allowed to invade and interfere with the revealed will of the Creator. It is aptly accomplished with the claim of there being no command for or against. The ideas of people are then processed through the avenue of an allegory.

This is to parallel the matter to some activity that isn't related to the actual commandment. To quote: the Bible tells us we are to go teach the word. How we go is our decision; by train, plane, or boat etc. There is an undeniable example of this problem in today's world of Christian faith and practice. In consideration of the problem that is so common, the study should start with the very beginning of the Lord's church.

The record is given of the early church. "...and they continued steadfastly in the apostles' doctrine and fellowship, and in breaking of bread, and in prayers. And fear came upon every soul: and many wonders and signs were done by the apostles. And all that believed were together, and had all things common; and sold their possessions and goods, and parted them to all men, as every man had need, and they, continuing daily with one accord in the temple, and breaking bread from house to house, did eat their meat with gladness and singleness of heart, praising God, and having favor with all the people. And the Lord added to the church daily such as should be saved. (Acts 2:42—47)

"And the multitude of them that believed were of one heart and of one soul: Neither said any of them that aught of the things which he possessed was his own; but they had all things common. And with great power gave the apostles witness of the resurrection of the Lord Jesus: and great grace was upon them all. Neither was there any among them that lacked: for as many as were possessors of lands or houses sold them, and brought the prices of the things that were sold, and laid them down at the apostles' feet; and distribution made unto every man according as he had need." (Acts 4:32-37)

This is a quick summary of the church in its infancy. The first eight chapters in the book of Acts tell of the church and its beginning. The design, arrangement, and procedure for the continuation of the church was formulated in this time of beginning growth and organization.

This was a time of extraordinary harmony and good-will among the faithful. It was a time of rapid increase in numbers beyond anything seen in church growth today. Since that time many attempts have been made to duplicate the unparalleled events of that period in the matters of fellowship, peaceful existence, and numerical growth.

One important point of the beginning of the church is mentioned in passing; but, this point isn't examined closely. That point is the matter of **infancy**. Although references are made to this as the time of **church infancy,** the points of infancy are not explored or investigated for content, meaning and application.

Looking closely at the elements shows that the church in its beginning can truly be compared to an infant in every way. It started very small and quickly grew to a great number in a seemingly short period of time. The Father provided care and watchful attention for the infant church which was no less than is required for the new born child.

Some of the details are easily apparent in that the new converts were provided with daily needs over a period of time. These needs included physical nourishment in addition to the expected spiritual sustenance. The necessary security for the infant was provided against possible outside physical harm.

The protection and spiritual nourishment was given though the work of the apostles. They were the shield and shepherds for the church. In the position of guardian, they were the targets for the threats and persecution. They were an example of endurance and perseverance until the church could become mature enough to endure hardship. (Acts 4 & 5)

For the damage that threatened from within the church, instant remedy was given from the loving and watchful Father. Acts 5:1-11 gives the account of the attempted entry of hypocrisy into the body of the infant church.

"But a certain man named Ananias, with Sapphira his wife, sold a possession, and kept back part of the price, his wife also being privy to it, and brought a certain part, and laid at the apostles' feet. But Peter said, Ananias, why hath Satan filled thine heart to lie to the Holy Spirit, and to keep back part of the price of the land? while it remained, was it not thine own? and after it was sold, was it not in thine own power? why hast thou conceived this thing in thine heart. Thou hast not lied unto men, but unto God. And Ananias hearing these words fell down, and gave up the ghost;" (Acts 5:1-11)

It is interesting to notice that the infant church also had the attention and interest of the general population much the same as any new born. Attention was focused on the infant church whether or not entrance into it was desired.

Everyone knew about it, and it was given due respect. "And they, continuing daily with one accord in the temple, . . .praising God and having favor with the people." "And of the rest durst no man join himself to them: but the people magnified them." (Acts 2:47, 5:13)

Along with every other provision for the infant church, a cradle was provided. The first thought in providing a cradle for an infant is to allow space for movement while giving protection from unwelcome intrusions, whether accidental or intentional. The allotted space is important for well being and growth. The cradle provides several necessary elements for an infant in the first year or two.

The first years of life for an infant revolve around the cradle. Here the babe is given a place of comfort and security. Security and calm are important for the time of rapid growth and development.

For the infant church, the cradle was the temple. In every sense of the word the temple was the cradle provided for the infant church by its loving Father. His temple was the birthright of the church because this was the place where God's people came together to hear God's law throughout times past.

The church, as the earthly manifestation of the eternal kingdom, was all the more entitled to the use of God's house. As the cradle is provided for an infant child, the temple was provided at this time in the history of the church without any forethought or effort on the part of the church itself.

The length of time the church continued to use the temple in Jerusalem was in relation to the needs of the developing church. There was time for the church to become fully organized with the plan clearly shown for future continuance. The temple was the appropriate cradle in regard to the infant church until all this could be accomplished.

The church was watched and cared for, with security maintained until the time it could mature in faith and strength. But, the temple was not the permanent headquarters for the church. The child must sometimes be compelled to leave its familiar and comfortable base. When time for change arrives, those of a mature physical stature are all the more difficult to persuade.

At this point the persecution began in earnest.

"And at that time there was a great persecution against the church which was at Jerusalem: and they were all scattered abroad throughout the regions of Judea and Samaria, except the apostles... Therefore they that were scattered abroad went every where preaching the word." (Acts 8:1-4)

From this time forward, the message is one of the church on the forward march, taking the gospel into all the world.

The Lord did not plan for the church to remain in the cradle. Daily provisions of food and care were not to continue indefinitely. (Compare with Acts 6:1-3 with II Thessalonians 3:10-12, and I Timothy 5:16) Neither the plan, nor the command is shown which tells of the church remaining in the temple or staying together for an infinite period of time as a group headquartered in Jerusalem.

There was never a lament in any of the epistles for the desire or expectation, to return to the first estate. If this had been the plan, there would have been no change. The child of God, the church of Christ, was not to remain in the cradle. The daily care and feeding would not be on a continuing basis. The Apostle Paul makes the issue simple in saying, ". . .that if any would not work neither should he eat. (II Thessalonians 3:10)

The provisions for infancy were finished. The time had come for the child to grow up and take responsibility. It was time to leave the cradle. Paul left no doubt in his message to the churches.

"For even when we were with you, this we commanded you, that if any would not work, neither should he eat. For we hear that there are some which walk among you disorderly, working not at all, but are busy bodies. Now them that are such we command and exhort by our Lord Jesus Christ, that with quietness they work, and eat their own bread," (II Thessalonians 3:10)

"But if any provide not for his own, and specially for those of his own house, he hath denied the faith, and is worse than an infidel." (I Timothy 5:8) During the infancy of the church, daily needs were provided for every new convert. (Read Acts 2:34-37, 44-45 6:1)

Since that time every effort has been made to reconstruct and continue the events of the beginning church. Believers of Christ are convinced that this time period in church history was the time of perfection. They believe it is necessary to duplicate every aspect of this period before the church will again be truly complete in the sight of God. As one man said, (These are) "the principles of our movement". In other words, the regaining of the infant form, condition, structure, and status; this is the vision, the ideal state of being? (Consider Luke 8:14, II Corinthians 13:9, Hebrew 6:1)

Attempts at instantly speaking foreign languages, communal or collective living, and miracle healings are some of the signs of the struggle to bring the church again to the infant state. It is thought that if the early beginnings of the church could be duplicated that all believers would again be "of one heart and one soul:" with the same exceptional growth in numbers. (Acts 4:32, Acts 21:30)

In the search for that perfect state, every religious group strives to maintain one common element. The one element is that of the cradle. People are under strong conviction that the centrally located building is the right thing to do. It is thought that the first Christians filled the requirement of a meeting place by meeting in the temple on a continuing basis. It is also reasoned that as the gospel spread, use was made of the Jewish synagogues in any given area.

As stated earlier, in the beginning of the church, the temple was where the church was begun. (Acts 2:46) This was the only place in the known world that worshipped the unseen God. People who were interested in correct and true worship would be found at this location.

But none should imagine that the temple was used by Christians for an indefinite period of time as an accepted practice. It is possible that the temple was denied to Christians as early as Acts 4:31. By this time Peter and John had been removed with force from the temple where they had healed the man lame from birth.

Scripture shows the Apostles going first to the Jews with the gospel message. The Jews were found in numbers in the temple and their synagogues. (17:1) But the attitude of the Jewish religious leaders toward the gospel of Christ and Christians, prohibits any idea of Christians ever meeting in Jewish synagogues. Remember the persecution by the man Saul in taking Christian men and women from their very houses? (Acts 8:3) Christians weren't safe anywhere, and surely not in the Jewish holy places. The written word never once speaks of Christians meeting in Jewish houses (synagogues) of worship.

Because the Jewish system had the temple and the synagogues for assembled worship, building programs are justified. This is some of the reasoning used in every discussion about church property. People are convinced that church property is a righteous necessity in the Christian dispensation. In actual fact the need for the church property is thought to be as necessary for the continuance of any particular denominational group as the Bible itself.

Where people see no specific Bible instructions for what they think are specific matters, they feel free to make the decisions and answer the questions. All, from the most liberal to the more conservative believers in Christ, believe that church property is an unavoidable obligation.

Recognizing the difference in beginning and continuing events of any Bible time period gives answers to many questions. In observing the various dispensations of time, each period began with happenings which were intended only for the beginning. The church is also portrayed with things unique to its beginning.

People often center their attention upon the obvious material things, more intriguing miracles, or mysterious events, to the neglect of equally compelling spiritual matters and every day continuance. The subtle course for future continuation is passed over in the rush toward the obvious. **The things**

which are permanent are not separated from things that are temporary.

The structural composition of the church was given when Jesus said,

"The kingdom of God cometh not with observation: neither shall they say, Lo here! or, lo there! for, behold, the kingdom of God is within you." (Luke 17:20-21)

Not, lo on Fifth and Main Streets or lo on the corner of Tenth and East Streets in a certain brick/stone structure with stained glass windows.

"Now therefore ye are no more strangers and foreigners, but fellow citizens with the saints, and of the household of God; and are built upon the foundation of the apostles and prophets, Jesus Christ himself being the chief corner stone: in whom all the building fitly framed together groweth unto a **holy temple** in the Lord: in whom ye also are builded together for a habitation of God through the Spirit." (Ephesians 2:19-22, I Peter 2:5)

This is the structural substance of the church as shown in God's written word.

Because the idea of the church building prevails, it is assumed that churches in every locality must provide a centrally located building for public worship. This is the 'necessary inference' which justifies the extensive outlay of money, time, and energy that is required for almost any architectural effort.

No argument can change the force of God's word. Christians are the structural substance of the church. As such they are to fellowship in assembling for worship. Because Christians are to meet together and worship with other Christians, most people presume this is a command that all Christians of any particular locality are to worship in one location. To do otherwise is to be judged as one that is unfaithful. In present day religious thinking, it is impossible to avoid the demand that as nearly as possible all Christians meet in one location.

In comparing this position with what Jesus told his disciples, the picture appears quite different. He said,

"For where two or three are gathered together in my name, there am I in the midst of them (Matthew 18:20)

Meeting in one location gives the appearance of strength and unity. Usually for a period of time, the unity and harmony seem to be all that it should or could possibly be. However, with human nature being what it is, the harmony and fellowship wears thin. Numerous and serious separations and groups appear in a very distinct way.

The Bible documentation of church history contains compelling examples of the church in action. There is a noticeable absence (silence) of set quotas for the number to be present for worship at any given time in any given locality.

In the strictest sense of the written Word, Christians are free to worship any place with any number of Christians. In the present religious environment the limits and demands are made by those in leadership positions.

In Bible examples, occasions arose when needs were met with the gathering together of the larger numbers of brethren. The occasions involved problems before the church or for purposes of common communion and fellowship. Witness the problem of false teachers entering the churches of Antioch in Acts 15. Verse 12 speaks of "the multitude" that was meeting in Jerusalem to consider the matter.

In this present society, it is not uncommon for multitudes to gather together on many different occasions for one reason or another. Sometimes the gatherings are in public facilities and sometimes in the open. It doesn't seem strange for this to happen until it applies to the church. Then it becomes necessary for the church to have facilities that will accommodate everyone in attendance.

Jesus said, "Foxes have holes, and birds of the air have nests; but the Son of man hath not where to lay his head." (Matthew 8:20) The church is the body of Christ. "...and gave him to be the head over all things to the church, which is his body, the fullness of him that filleth all in all." It does not seem reasonable that God would provide for the body what he did not provide for the Head.

When sending the disciples to preach the coming of the kingdom, Jesus said,

"Provide neither gold, nor silver, nor brass in your purses; nor scrip for your journey, neither two coats, neither shoes, nor yet staves: for the workman is worthy of his meat...The disciple is not above his master, nor the servant above his Lord." (Matthew 10:9-10, 24)

In the gospel, in the faith of Christ, Christians today appear to be above their Lord. Yet with all the material wealth, there is no comparison. Jesus and his disciples accomplished more than can be written in words. All this was accomplished with none of the structural resources imagined necessary by the mind of today's believers.

The inclination to build is innate in the human race. When honor is due the honorable, construction begins in the form of buildings, streets, monuments, or ornaments, to name a few. The church building is considered by the congregation an effort to honor God as each group is able to provide. But this worship, this honor is one that goes beyond the bounds of the faith and doctrine of God's revealed will. (II John 9)(Amplified New Testament)

Much is required in funding when the Church owns and maintains a house for purposes of a meeting place. The financing of the meeting place is one of the greatest out-lays of funds for most religious groups. The result is the building becomes the focal point around which every church member and activity is centered. In the final analysis these things are the greater part of the ties that bind.

The Apostle Paul gives instruction involving several issues among the brethren. But the subjects of managing, financing and building of structures are sorely neglected. There is silence.

Finances and management are discussed in the epistles with no loose ends left to the imagination. The Apostle wrote about collective funds on several occasions. Included in these instructions is an important element that isn't given attention. This element is the fact that as the need arose, collections and distributions were conducted. Distributions for each collection were specific and timely. There were no funds sitting in the bank collecting interest.

The collective funds and their purposes are listed in three categories with strict instructions and guidelines. The first of these is listed as care for the saints in need with the first duty of the church being the nurturing of itself. This was the first large distribution of funds and supplies shown among the early Christians. Everything about the occasion and the way it was handled served a logical purpose and filled the need. (Romans 15:25-26)

The next distribution of funds within the church is in support of those who give full attention to preaching the gospel. The apostles are the best examples of this effort and the respect it deserves.

"For the Scripture saith, Thou shalt not muzzle the ox that treadeth out the corn. And the laborer is worthy of his reward." (I Corinthians 9:9, I Timothy 5:18)

The third distribution is to be for widows that are destitute, with no resources or family members. These are to be women who are devoted to Christ and serve in that capacity. (I Timothy 5:3-16) Even this is not shown to be a collection into a treasury. The church treasury is not a subject of enlightenment from within the New Testament. Funds were delivered promptly after the collection for the intended purpose.

"...providing for honest things, not only in the sight of the Lord, but also in the sight of men"

The continuing treasury is, by its very nature, a behind-the-scene activity, under the control (and temptation of one or more people.

These three areas are the distributions for which the church, as a body, is responsible. Included is instruction for the purpose these collections are to fulfill, to whom the benefit belongs and how it is to be carried out. The issue of church resources being used for maintaining church property is a matter of secular history, not found nor verified in the Scripture.

The New Testament church met for worship in individual homes or in buildings already existing or in the open air. These meeting places are shown in the book of Acts and in the letters to the churches.

"And daily in the temple, and in every house, they ceased not to teach and preach Jesus Christ." (Acts 5:42): And on the Sabbath we went out of the city by a riverside, where prayer was wont to be made; and we sat down, and spake unto the women which resorted thither." (Acts 16:13)

"And upon the first day of the week, when the disciples came together to break bread, Paul preached unto them, ready to depart on the morrow; and continued his speech until midnight and there were many lights in the upper chamber, where they were gathered together." (Acts 20:7-8)

"...he departed from them, and separated the disciples, disputing daily in the school of one Tyrannus. And this continued by the space of two years; so that all they which dwelt in Asia heard the word of the Lord Jesus, both Jews and Greeks. (Acts 19:9)

"And Paul dwelt two whole years in his own hired house, and received all that came in unto him, preaching the kingdom of God, and teaching those things which concern the Lord Jesus Christ, with all confidence, no man forbidding him." (Acts 28:30-31)

Paul maintained his own hired house from the resources received for his on-going work in the gospel. (Philippians 4:14-18) Paul was an old man and a prisoner at this time. This was the way he used the financial resources at his disposal to preach the gospel in the particular set of circumstances he was in.

"Greet Priscilla and Aquila, my helpers in Christ Jesus.. .Likewise greet the church that is in their house." (Romans 16:3-5)

The last chapter of Romans, when studied slowly and carefully, will show a revealing view of the church in its onward movement. The church house is not mentioned.

These are some of the examples left to us that leave no doubt of the conditions of worship or the circumstances. The building funds and programs were nonexistent in the plan and purpose of those sent to bring the gospel to the world in Bible times. Again, in every dispensation of time, required events are present in any beginning process. Because of their very nature, it was not possible for the special occurrences of the beginning process to remain as an overall part of the continuing course.

As the beginning process was working, guidelines were set in motion for the continuation of the working order from that time forward. Because of this, every beginning contains elements which come to an end. This then allows the ultimate concept to develop, mature, and become fully useful. We can't imagine leaving the scaffolding up around the building after it is completed, even though it might come in handy when it is time for maintenance or window washing. The Lord's work also does not retain the first works of the first beginning.

During the time of the developing church, the Apostle Paul wrote,

"For we know in part, and we prophesy in part, but when that which is perfect is come, then that which is in part shall be done away. When I was a child, I spake as a child, I understood as a child, I thought as a child: but when I became a man, I put away childish things," (I Corinthians 13:9-11)

The building is thought to be necessary for purposes of an atmosphere of reverence and a separation from the outside intrusion of everyday life. Yet, with all the supposed material needs, the spirit of reverence and worship must come from within the heart. External material influences are not a part of the Christian fellowship. The worship of our God is not material based.

Regardless of the facts of the silence of the Bible in furnishing neither the command nor the plan for church property, some passages are a problem for those demanding such. Most of these passages are found in the book of I Corinthians, chapters 11 and 14. The following phrases are used to show that the Bible supports building programs.

"For first of all, when ye come together in the church..." I Corinthians 11:18

"When ye come together therefore into one place... "I Corinthians 11:20

"What! have ye not houses to eat and to drink in?" I Corinthians 11:20

"Wherefore, my brethren, When ye come together to eat, (the Lord's Supper) tarry one for another. And if any man hunger, let him eat at home; that ye come not together unto condemnation." I Corinthians 11:33—34

"...yet in the church I had rather speak five words..." I Corinthians 14:19.

"If therefore the whole be come together into one place... "I Corinthians 14:23

- .when ye come together..." I Corinthians 14.26

". . .let him keep silence in the church.. ."I Corinthians 14:28

"How is it then brethren? when ye come together, every one of you hath a psalm, hath a doctrine, hath a tongue, hath a revelation, hath an interpretation. Let all things be done unto edifying." I Corinthians 14:26

"And if they will learn anything, let them ask their husbands at home:... "I Corinthians 14:35

Surface reading of these passages may have significant indications for the anxious or overly inspired person. To the easily persuaded natural mind, it sounds as though we had better build a place of worship quickly before we become confused and find ourselves not knowing what we are doing or when it is to be done. It seems a simple thing to forget "that where two or three are gathered together in my name, there am I in the midst of them." (Matthew 18:20.)

Feelings and desires of the natural mind move in quickly in the problem of collective worship. In this situation human nature fails to notice that many activities are accomplished in one material location every day. Worship to God is one separate and discernible activity. (John 4:23-24)

True worshippers are able and content to worship in spirit and in truth. .. ."that he would grant you, according to the riches of his glory, **to be strengthened with might by his Spirit in the inner man:**" (Ephesians 3:16)

The same thinking of the natural man that led David to the decision to build a house for the ark of God are at work in the requirement of church property. We like David, see pressing needs where God has not so decreed. The human conscience imagines that because we live in this or that standard of housing there is the necessity for a house of worship to God that is of equal or better standard.

Guilt is created about many things in areas that have no resemblance to the commands of God. Spiritual guilt is easily created where there is lack of thoughtful spiritual knowledge. There is much of this type of guilt created in the religious world.

All of us have had experiences with someone seeking to place guilt or create fear to gain an advantage to themselves. These tactics are used in the business world every day. When false fear or guilt is used in spiritual realms, the results lead to eternal loss.

False guilt is the deadly force that knows no bounds for self destruction. It is a sensitivity touched by another that allows us to destroy our own effectiveness. Guilt is a means of control one may gain over another. This means is easily created by other people and also from within ourselves. Much of the time there is no awareness of false guilt. It must be one of Satan's favorite weapons. II Corinthians 7:10 speaks to the effects created by false guilt. This topic is not included in your usual discussion or labeled as a valid entity. If it were, people might begin to question their religious doctrine.

It serves very well as a solid distraction from true repentance of true guilt. In the use made of false guilt, the catch word is, "If you cannot defeat, then distract". The tactic works well in many areas of life. Especially is this true in the religious and/or spiritual realm. Also, with the natural inclination to build, it is not too difficult to turn this natural compulsion into a spiritual necessity.

And yet, church real estate serves the purposes of righteousness about as well as the broad phylacteries and long prayers of the Pharisees. (Matthew 23:5, 14) These worshippers had ready access to the most marvelous building of worship anywhere in the world. But, they were in rebellion to God to the overwhelming degree of murdering His only begotten Son.

In seeing pressing needs outside the revealed will of God, a false sense of guilt is easily created. David exhibited a sense of guilt about the difference in his great house of cedar as it compared to the tent of the tabernacle. In this he did not seem to realize he was belittling the plan of God. It is not uncommon for people to reason that they have a better plan "for this day and time".

It is common practice for ambitious religious leaders to use the position of leadership and the gift of persuasion to further their own ideas. Very few people take thought to question or investigate personal motives and intentions of those they think are trustworthy. Most people find it easy to simply agree with what seems to be a good idea. The majority of people do not question or risk confrontation with what seems reasonable or the majority view.

"Let no man beguile you of your reward in a voluntary humility and worshipping of angels, intruding into those things which he hath not seen, vainly puffed up by his fleshly mind." (Colossians 2:18). The creation of church property is a voluntary humility. It is certain that it isn't the type of humility that is commanded from God the Father.

The Lord Jesus died for the eternal soul of man. Eternal souls of mortal beings make up the eternal kingdom. The eternal kingdom is the church. The church is the purchased possession paid for with the blood of the Son of God.

"Take heed therefore unto yourselves, and to all the flock, over the which the Holy Spirit hath made overseers, to feed the church of God, which he hath purchased with his own blood." (Acts 20:28)

It does not stand as sound doctrine that the purchased possession, the spiritual body of Jesus Christ, is designed and destined to devote such an overwhelming degree of energies and resources to that which is purely temporal in nature. It does not stand as spiritual righteousness that unseen things of the invisible God are so overwhelmingly dependant upon the seen and purely carnal. (Ephesians 2:19-22, I Peter 2:4-8)

Much in time, planning and effort is required to continue a decidedly materialistic effort. There is no getting away from the needs of the church building, the payments, utilities and continual maintenance connected with said property. Every member is expected to meet at this place and contribute at this place. If they do not, they are regarded as something less than faithful. In the final analysis, the church pivots on the money point.

"And through covetousness shall they with feigned words make merchandise of you:" (II Peter 2:3)

The Faith of the Lord Jesus Christ makes no provision for blatant material profit at the expense of the church.

It is feared that the number of people would not increase if worship were conducted in the various homes. For sure, it wouldn't be as easy to keep tabs on the head count. It is a fact of religious life that the church building is a large part of the glue that holds the people together. Therefore people would tend to shy away from the Church that has no material based sign of existence.

Without the material property, the spiritual body does not exist in the eyes of the world. People have become conditioned to demands outside the law of Christ to the point that the simple things shown in the written Word appear unrealistic.

According to the standards that religious people have set for themselves, the Church building is proof that the church merits recognition as a valid religious body.

"For do I now persuade men, or God? or do I seek to please men? For if I yet pleased men, I should not be the servant of Christ. (Galatians 1:10)

It is feared that if it were not for the church building, many would not continue their faith. There is little doubt that this would happen. In actual fact, their faith is based in the size of the group and their property. The necessity causing the requirement for church property is created by fear and mistrust. This is fear of each other; the fear that each one won't maintain faith without careful scrutiny from other church members.

For other souls, church property contributes heavily to delinquency. With everyone meeting each and every time at one location, routine and boredom sets in. The big struggle, the excitement of a new building is finished. The part of life related to the Church becomes sure and comfortable. It is then easy to think there are enough people present for worship services that one or two won't be missed. In this type of setting, apathy sets in with increasing frequency. The joys of the former warmth and closeness turns into regiment and routine.

The Church as a whole finds groups separating from each other for reason of natural variations in occupation, social, and age differences. Insult and hurt often ensues. Meeting in one place does not guarantee spiritual joy or spiritual growth.

Where all the membership meets at one place at every appointed time, any problem that may arise, instantly affects every member in some way. If the problem should be kept quiet, then doubts arise about the spiritual brotherhood of the particular group. From these problems comes division into groups that exhibit anything but Christian attitudes toward differing views.

In the expectation that every member meet in one central location, difficulties are created for the physically weak and ill. They are cut off from worship for no fault of their own. In some instances of an extended illness, they never again worship with those of like faith. They are automatically denied fellowship because they are convinced that being present at the appointed place is the only acceptable way.

When all meet regularly at one place, family units are separated into separate study situations. The study subjects aren't brought together for common consideration. Then the family becomes dependant upon the regular teaching facilities to do their duty for them. Undue burdens are placed on class teachers to do for family members what they should be doing for themselves. This is an essential part of family relations that is set aside by those who claim it is for the good of all concerned.

The family responsibility to teach itself tends to become diluted and less intense. Spiritual family fellowship has much greater opportunity to become neglected. Individuals may know this should not be the case, but will allow it to happen as a matter of readily available convenience. From the one central point of separation the ever widening gulf is glaringly evident in every family.

As a matter of convenience, excessive expectations are placed on the local preacher. He must come up with at least two good sermons per week that will somehow, keep everyone awake for the time allotted for preaching each lesson. People expect the preacher to be thought provoking and inspiring in his presentation. But then because each individual did not search out and study the greater depths for himself, or was asleep, the thought provoking sermon is soon forgotten.

As a result of common practice, the preacher is expected to be college educated, therefore more knowledgeable in the word of God. But, in the correct situation, all Christians are to strive to be as capable as the minister in understanding and teaching the Scripture, with or without extensive education.

It is forgotten that it is written,

"For ye see your calling, brethren, how that not many wise men after the flesh, not many mighty, not many noble, are called:" (I Corinthians 1:26)

Despite this admonition, the preacher must have a degree to be recognized as credible and qualified to hold the position of minister.

In its own way this practice sets the minister in a separate position apart from the remaining brethren. He is held as counselor, comforter, and general authority in life and living by virtue of his position as minister. According to general practice the minister is expected to be available to everyone in the church for whatever need they feel is his responsibility. This is especially true in smaller groups. The minister has responsibilities toward the membership that are not expected of any other member, simply because he is the preacher. As a direct result, the duties of the evangelistic work are diminished considerably. In this position there is the comparison of a king over his own little kingdom.

By design and purpose, every Christian is duty bound to edify himself and those around him, including the evangelist. By design and purpose the man that "labors in word and doctrine" is to be free to preach the gospel to the lost.

"But watch thou in all things, endure afflictions, do the work of an evangelist, make full proof of thy ministry." (II timothy 4:5)

Rather than doing the work of an evangelist, the preacher is doing the work of an elder, and/or deacon. He serves in this office and often without the qualifications demanded in the Scripture.

Christians are to provoke themselves and each other in love and good works and financially support the spread of the gospel. Every Christian is indebted to Christ Jesus to be as willing and spiritually capable as any minister. Each is on common ground with the same opportunities for growth in the Faith. Instead the preacher is financially supported so he can supply the congregation in the spiritual matters which they should be supplying for themselves.

Little by little the face and function of every facet of the Faith and Doctrine of Christ is changed with one beginning point.

The family is the parallel to the church, and the church is a family in every way.

"Rebuke not an elder (older man), but entreat him as a father; and the younger men as brethren; and the elder women as mothers; the younger as sisters, with all purity." (I Timothy 5:1)

In its complete sense, the family is composed of several units with the fathers, mothers, children, aunts, uncles, cousins and grandparents. Ideally, everyone is available to everyone else for good times and bad. In the day to day flow of life, face to face contact for the entire family, is not based and set on a regular schedule.

Each family unit is self sufficient in normal daily situations. It should be no different for the several church families, whom ever this may come to include, outside or inside the immediate daily family relations, at any particular time or location of worship.

Modern times call for modern methods with up-dated ideas. The numerous advantages of church property have long been proclaimed. It is not uncommon for the created to think they have a better plan than the Creator, "for this day and time".

Because property and structures seem unquestionably bound to spiritual matters, people consider it a thing bordering on heresy to entertain any doubt for the commonly accepted standards and long held practices. Any other possibility appears impossible and unthinkable.

Because the matter of church property isn't listed as a "thou shalt" or "thou shalt not", it is considered appropriate for men to make these decisions. People are convinced that as long as this does not conflict with a clearly stated command, violates no moral conduct, and appears to be the expedient thing to do, they are then free to use their own judgment. Adding to God's revealed word is not seen as an actual transgression when Church owned real estate is involved.

Church property must be classed as either a spiritual matter or a carnal matter. There can be no question of this being a carnal, material matter. The question then demands an answer as to why the spiritual body of Christ should be so heavily dependent upon material means for spiritual survival? Why should the spiritual body of Jesus go outside the spiritual Word in its efforts? Where is the great benefit other than to cause the Church to "also be like all the nations (churches) round about us"? (Deuteronomy 17:14-20)

According to human standards it would indeed be a social/emotional embarrassment for church people who do not own a Church building. It isn't a spiritual embarrassment. Therefore it must be something other than commandment from Scripture that holds people so strongly to the matter of material demands.

Christians are commanded to thoroughly investigate every matter relating to worship and service to God.

"I beseech you therefore, brethren, by the mercies of God, that ye present your bodies a living sacrifice, holy, acceptable unto God, which is your reasonable service. **And be not conformed to this world:** but be ye transformed by the renewing of your mind, that ye may **prove** what is that good, and acceptable, and perfect will of God." (Romans 12:1-2)

This Scripture does not speak only to individual conduct but to the church as a whole. The church that would be guided by worldly standards, is also condemned or judged with the world. Note Matthew 7:21 which speaks of believers who were (are) to be rejected.

Yet with determination, and in the face of silence in the Scriptures, the issue of church property is deemed as a materially conditional thing of unquestioned necessity. This is the mind of the world. This is the mind of every recognized religious body. But it is written, ". . .for that which is highly esteemed among men is abomination in the sight of God." (Luke 16:16)

The worship and purpose of the church is spiritual and the achievements are guided according to Word of the Spirit. The church in its true sense is as spiritual in comparison to the tabernacle as the tabernacle is carnal (material) in comparison to the church. (Hebrews 9:1-28)

There are marks of infancy and there are marks of maturity for the church as well as for the child. Those manifestations tell who is being dealt with and on what level.

"And he said unto me, My grace is sufficient for thee: for my strength is made perfect in weakness. Most gladly therefore will I rather glory in my infirmities, that the power of Christ may rest upon me. Therefore I take pleasure in infirmities, in reproaches, in necessities, in persecutions, in distresses for Christ's sake: for when I am weak, then am I strong." (II Corinthians 12:7-10)

In the eyes of the religious world, the group that would not maintain the expected norm in church property would indeed appear to be weak and insignificant.

"Are ye so foolish? having begun in the Spirit, are ye now made perfect by the flesh?" (Galatians 3:3)

The command is that Christians must worship in spirit and in truth. This does not say worship must be done in a certain building location.

"God that made the world and all things therein seeing that he is Lord of heaven and earth, dwelleth not in temples made with hands; neither is worshipped with men's hands, as though he needed anything, seeing he giveth to all life, and breath, and all things;" (Acts 17:24-25)

The opinions of men about the options of men lead to expediencies for which the Word of God makes no allowances and offers no hope of reward.

"According as his divine power hath given unto us all things that pertain unto life and godliness, through the knowledge of him that hath called us unto glory and virtue," and, **"Whosoever transgresseth, and abideth not in the doctrine of Christ hath not God."** (II Peter 1:3, II John 9)

Church owned property is an idea that comes only from the minds of men. Necessities that cause the need for Church property also comes only from the minds of men. Sacrifices to God which are made according to the minds of men have only the promises of men. Therefore the Christian is not obligated before God in the problem of church ownership of lands and structures. The Silence of God's Word must prevail.

A Final Word

Thorough comprehension often takes concentrated effort to achieve complete understanding of these subjects. For most people the effort is too much and they let themselves be thoroughly convinced of their doctrinal position and its completeness. Within the confines of this position the new convert is invited to investigate certain things within restricted bounds. It is expected that most doctrinal issues be accepted without question, investigation, or greater depth and expansion beyond the accepted norm. It is interesting to note also, that often the boundaries are expected to be more or less automatically understood.

Certain fundamental doctrines claim to avoid human based traditions. Yet, in reality, there are set patterns and standards of faith and personal conduct that stifles individual investigation and expression.

The point of view was appropriately expressed by a young man named Joe Molino, in saying, "The reason most people come to this Church is because of dissatisfaction with their own doctrine in some point, or their preacher, or church in general". The statement was further made that for anyone truly interested in change, to find themselves in yet another position of merely accepting another form of human tradition, is a source of disappointment; that the Bible needed to be open and free, for discussion on any issue the heart may have a need.

Upon accepting membership in some churches, the new convert quickly learns that the members in general are set in their beliefs and your only choice is to accept their viewpoint. People from other belief systems seek out the congregations claiming to teach the one true faith of the Bible. Disappointment then comes in the realization that there is no basic difference.

These Churches profess to their new converts a freedom to question, investigate and to inquire in their studies of the Scripture. However, any such actions are met with a rigid repudiation. The need of the convert to know the basis of any point of doctrine, "isn't with the intention of changing the Word of Jesus". The need is to know for self assurance the teaching of the doctrines of the Churches and where they were based from the beginning".

The new convert has been led to believe that, Truth has nothing to fear from investigation. With this, the convert comes into these Churches hearing that, "they teach thus saith the Lord for all they say and do". They say their purpose is to "do Bible things in Bible ways". It is a rude awakening to find that one is expected to fit into the accepted mold with no forceful, persistent, questioning or an over abundant curiosity.

This work is presented as a probe into these long term beliefs and the related Scriptures. The chief intent of this effort is to seek the purest form of the principle within the Revealed Word, in relation to these subjects.

The effort to find salvation is as a road which is traveled. Salvation, like the road, is a way, a path which is prepared. The road isn't designed and constructed in accordance with personal ideas as we travel.

Salvation, like a highway, has markers along the way. These markers serve to reassure the traveler that the route is correct. Markers also serve to prevent the accidental straying onto a side road. To avoid or overlook any of these markers is to take a wrong turn and miss the way.

Along every highway there are many side roads and attractions which seek to gain the attention of the traveler. This is more true for those traveling the road to eternal salvation. There are many blind alleys and misleading directions which are offered to any who would sincerely seek to find the one true way.

One of the most reassuring events on the road to salvation is to know the correct route is found. Even with knowing the route is undeniably correct, it is possible to stop along the way. Then progress is halted short of the destination and deviation is made just before entrance. To those who are traveling this road, the satisfaction is great.

The subjects discussed in this effort are some of the road markers that are missed. Most people seem to think these markers aren't important. Some of the points aren't considered as having true or significant bearing on the issues relative to the quest for salvation.

Because these things aren't thought to be important, they have been met with various degrees of indifference, hostility, mockery and friendly jesting. But none of these attitudes answer the questions or fill the need to follow the commands of Jesus as Lord. These attitudes also do not excuse anyone from accountability.

"All the commandments which I commanded thee this day shall ye observe to do,...that he might make thee know that man doth not live by bread only, but by **every** word that proceedeth out of the mouth of the Lord." (Deuteronomy 8; 1-5, Luke 4:4)

Paul wrote, "Now we have received, not the spirit of the world, but the Spirit which is of God; that we might know the things that are freely given to us of God. Which things also we speak, not in the words which man's wisdom teacheth, but which the Holy Spirit teacheth comparing spiritual things with spiritual. But the natural man réceiveth not the things of the Spirit of God; for they are foolishness unto him: neither can he know them, because they are spiritually discerned."(I Corinthians 2:12—14)

The things undertaken in this study seek to show Bible teachings that are neglected by those hoping to find salvation through Jesus Christ, the Saviour of the world. This is the same Jesus who spoke of his second coming beginning in Matthew 24:36.

"But of that day and hour knoweth no man, no, not the angels of heaven, but my Father only. But as the days of Noah were, so shall also the coming of the Son of man be. For as in the days that were before the flood they were eating and drinking, marrying and giving in marriage, until the day that Noah entered into the ark, and knew not until the flood came, and took them all away; so shall also the coming of the Son of man be."

"But as the days of Noah were, so shall also the coming of the Son of man be. For as in the days that were before the flood they were,"... (teaching that all one had to do is believe in God and build the ark of their choice and they would be saved, and that they should not be concerned with the minor details that God had given for the building of the ark or of believing there was only one ark that would save them).

There surely were people that honored and respected Noah up to a point. There were some who believed some of what Noah had to say but not quite all he had to say. There were those who were concerned about the decay of the world around them. But, like people of today, they to could have thought that an honest and sincere spirit was all that was required.

Some could have believed what Noah taught of the great flood and thought the idea of the ark could possibly have some merit. But then comes the matter of: "Who does Noah think he is in believing he is the only one who can build an ark?" or, "We want something that looks a little brighter and more cheerful so we will build our own ark". In every age and time there are differing amounts of disbelief from the nearest to the farther most degree.

"But as in the days of Noah were, so shall also the coming of the Son of man be." Men have designed and built every kind of religion possible with some so closely resembling the church found in Scripture, that it is very difficult to distinguish them as not quite complete. In conjunction with the discrepancies, there are strong and self assured assertions that the whole truth is presented. These discrepancies are the things that are brought forward in this study.

In the world of the various religions, it is a game played for the seeking soul, the needy spirit, by those who would profit for power and money.

Do we continue to make a toy of God's Word and a mockery of the love of Christ and His sacrifice, or do we search out the truth? Every word of God is given for a purpose. Nothing is to be discredited or discounted.

Any single thing brought into the Faith aside from the revealed Word, be it small or great, is to bring in the corruption of the world. Let us beware, for eternity is final. (II Peter 1:4)

It is primary we remember that without repentance from sin and all the attendant wickedness, no amount of faith, prayer, baptism and good works is going to save the soul in eternity. Without repentance we are never able to obey the spiritual commands of confession, baptism, prayer and meditation. God is the only one qualified to properly define and identify sin and the remedy.

Religion is a security blanket. Fear of investigating religious beliefs leaves people stymied and unable to search for truth. This book is just one search.

"But the **fearful**, and unbelieving, and the abominable, and murders, and whoremongers, and sorccers, and idolators, and all liars shall have their part in the lake which burneth with fire and brimstone: which is the second death". (Revelations 21:8)

Religion is easy to find, either from within ourselves or created by other individuals. The promises of God come only through the faith which is the doctrine of Christ.

May God's Grace Be With You

F. Steward Bartlett devoted more than twenty years to the research and study into these points of doctrine which most theologians pointedly ignore and refuse to investigate. She now resides in Northwest Arizona.

www.ingramcontent.com/pod-product-compliance
Lightning Source LLC
Chambersburg PA
CBHW032104090426
42743CB00007B/233